Fireside

PRAISE for EAT MANGOES NAKED

"SARK reminds us that pleasure is no extravagance-rediscovering the child within and connecting to the pleasures of just being."
Luchina Fisher, Contributing Editor
The Oprah Magazine

"SARK makes us realize what's important in life - more pleasure, joy, love and mangoes!"
-Marc Allen, author of *Visionary Business*

"This book is soul food. It is an invitation to grow into the shoes you were meant to dance in."
-Cristina Carlino
CEO philosophy
Author of *The Rainbow Connection*

OTHER BOOKS BY SARK

A creative companion
inspiration sandwich
Living Juicy
SARK's Journal : Play! Book
The Magic Cottage Address Book
Succulent Wild Woman
The Bodacious Book of Succulence
Change your life without Getting out of Bed
Transformation Soup

eAT
MaNGOeS
NAKeD

FiNDiNG PLeASuRe everyWHeRe
and
Dancing with the Pits!

BY SARK

A Fireside BOOK
PUBLiSHed By SiMon & SCHUSTeR
new YORK ♡ lonDon ♡ SYDney ♡ Singapore

Copyright 2001 By SARK

Created By SARK

ISBN: 0-684-85977-7

CIP: 00-066258

Fireside
rockefeller center
1230 Ave of the Americas
New York, NY 10020

Manufactured and
printed God bless the printers!
in our United States of
America

10 9 8 7 6 5 4 3 2 1

Thanks to
All the
sales reps!

Photo credits Thank you!
Page 193 #1 Tim Hyde
#2 Kim Indresano/Muse
Page 195... Rodney Julian Jackson
Page 191... Wade Jacobson

Special Thanks to Jennifer Wright
for subtitle assistance + Brilliance

THANKS TO:
SIMON & SCHUSTER
Trish Todd: Bless your editing!
Marcela Landres: for All the Assistance!
Cherlynne Li: sensitive art direction
Jim Thiel: enduring production
Faren Bachelis: Gifted copy editor

THANKS TO:
andrea scher:
special eyes
for grace +
buoyancy in
production
so GREAT

CAMPSARK:
To Adrienne
steele, Brigette
scheel for
SUPPORT
so many
Dimensions

Thanks to
London
King
for
sublime
publicity

THANKS TO:
creative culture
Debra Goldstein:
for Literary support and
jetski: driving
Mary ann Naples:
for gifts of Literature
and kind eyes

Thank you to the eugene registered Guard Wayne eastburn
eye to page 150

THIS BOOK is DeDICATED TO:
PATRICIA HuntinGTON

WHO HAS SO elegantly Assisted Me in
Finding My True pleasure in THE
MIDST of All the pits!

TO:

Deliciously,

eAT MaNGOes

nAKeD

THESE ARe DABS of pleAsure for your DAYS and nights!

THE
TRAVELING
DREAM CHAIR...
CURL UP
Close your
eyes...
You and
Your Traveling
Dream
Chair
Will
FloAT
THROUGH
Spaces
To
Brand
new
Places

SING
A
SONG
of
Surrender

leAve Your BAGS

Lift Your Self

UP

I KNOW HOW FASCINATING THE
BAGGAGE can Be...
you can still put it Down

MAGICAL
BATHOTUB

SLip in,
close Your eyes
and You will FiND
A Spot
to Dive DowN
into
THAT leADS
TO A tropical
PARADiSe

All For You!

EAT MANGOES NAKED
FINDING PLEASURE EVERYWHERE
DANCING WITH and THE PITS!

Mango Love

BY SARK

THIS BOOK is A traveling pleasure companion, and A reminder to seek out pleasure and LIGHTly scoop it up!

It is Also A guide to Finding pleasure in All of the difficult places: During illness, AT THE periodontist, FACING our AGING and MORTALITY, and All THE cHALLENGes of BEing Human.

PLEASURE and JOY Live in All of THE corners and crevices too, not JUST BRIGHT SUNLIGHT. We MUST learn To cultivate pleAsure and invite it into All the plAces in our Lives, no MATTer WHAT else is HAPPening.

IT is our Birthright to enjoy our-
selves and Find All The pleasure in
Our Lives. Pleasure Loves Company
and Delights in Being Discovered.
   I Frequently Forget About pleasure.
It is easy To Become Consumed By
(Work) and By (Doing)...

WHere's THe pleasure?

   Pleasure Can Be So elusive, MoMenTARy
and SerenDipitous. We Can CHASE it
AWAy By Trying To plan it, GraB it,
Clutch it or orcHestrate it.
   We Can Dance THrough our Lives
and still Be "responsiBle."
   We Can Dive Deeply into our
CHAllenGes, and still CHortle with
Glee.

(let's CHortle More!)

let's loosen our clothes, and
practice illuminated decadence
and conscious luxury.

let's live more in pleasure and
bring pleasure to others. pleasure can
escort us safely through very
difficult times and give our spirits
a place to replenish.

Pleasure and joy invite our best
selves out to play and quiet our
critical voices. They give us a much-
needed place to creatively refill.

(Then we can truly help others)

Pleasure definitely multiplies as we
share it.

THIS BOOK is:
A leaping treasure trove of
pleasures
an exuberant burst of good energy
A companion for very dark days

A guide to giving and receiving pleasure, (permission) for pleasure, vicarious pleasures, joy in the midst of pain, pleasure mentors and lots of ways to activate:

More pleasure and JOY in your life and others' lives.

Let's truly treasure our days and nights, moving through light and dark, sitting with our pain and fear, and welcoming our joy.

We so often try to present our ideal or best selves to the world. Let me invite you into the pleasures of sharing your

Fragile, wrinkled, dented, tiniest self!

I assure you, it's what people find most endearing about you!

I invite you
into
expanded pleasure
and
Trve joy in all that it is to be Human... especially the unacknowledged parts.

Pleasure no matter what else is happening.

I will share my process, lessons failings, discoveries and blessings with you.

let's proceed into
PleAsure...

note: There is a lot of pleasure in eating mangoes naked or... just thinking about it! 15

CLUSTERS of
ANGELS

ALL ALONG
YOUR PATH
WHEREVER YOU GO
THERE ARE
CLUSTERS OF ANGELS
ON A MISSION
THESE ANGELS
SURROUND YOUR SOUL
WHEREVER YOU GO
WHATEVER HAPPENS

Permission for Pleasure

We Deserve JOY and pleasure! They Are the whole point of Being Human. Yet creating and receiving pleasure is elusive for so Many, WHY?

Myself included

Many of us Are More comfortable with and Accustomed to pAin or punishment.

Pleasure is THOUGHT of As Accidental, or A Bonus THAT we can't count on. It is true THAT pleasure can Be elusive if we insist on it in A rigid WAY.

Remember your pArents SAYing, "we came on this VACATion To Have Fun and you're Going To Have it!"

And we Do it to ourselves, Setting up social engagements or events, And Then WATCHing THe pleasure DrAin AWAY Due to MOOD or circumstance.

Down The DrAin...

KnowFun

I HAD this experience recently with pleasure. I Found myself riding A serious wave of pleasure for About 4 DAYS, which showed no sign of ending.

serious wave of pleasure

I Began Feeling scared AT THE Amount of JOY I WAS experiencing, and noticed Myself creating DRAMA, Almost Like putting THE Brakes on pleasure.

THe struggle still Feels More comFortABle TO Me THan the pleasure, and I wonder How I can extend or expand the pleasure?

I think THAT one of the wAYs is TO CHange THe Formula.

if we SAY, for exAmple:

prickly grass THAT itches

Going to A concert = pleAsure WE MIGHT FIND: prickly GRASS, WARM BeverAGes, poor sound systems, Belligerent Fans or offensive Lyrics.

WE COULD CHANGE THE FORMULA to:
GOING to A CONCERT = A TIME
   INSTEAD of GOING to HAVE "A GOOD TIME"
(WHICH CAN CAUSE PRESSURE or STRUGGLE), WE
MIGHT JUST HAVE A "TIME."
   THIS ALLOWS OUR ACTUAL EXPERIENCE
TO OCCUR.
   MAYBE WE'LL GET TO THE CONCERT, AND
LEAVE AFTER 10 MINUTES. MAYBE WE'LL SEE
A SIGN THAT SAYS "FRESH PEACHES"
AND STOP to BUY DOZENS,
AND GIVE THEM AWAY.

   MAYBE WE'LL STOP
THE CAR, AND HAVE
OUR OWN HOMEMADE
CONCERT BY THE river,
SINGING off KEY.
   PLEASURE loves
SURPRISE AND SPONTANEOUS
EXPRESSION!

To give ourselves permission for
pleasure means moving in new directions,
with no expectations and changing our
moods in the process.

we need to change moods
like clothes

I AM now giving
you new permission for pleasure. you can
use THis whenever you Feel stuck, lost, or
out of pleasure

Brand—new permission slip

p l e a s u r e

is All Around you

it Doesn't leave you. you leave it

STep ForwArd
into new JOY
or
sit and experience THe present Moment

reminder: pleAsure can Appear very QuickLy

Perspectives of Pleasure

It is important to recognize where pleasure is and how it shows itself, in order to expand your vision of pleasure.

WHAT MIGHT you see if you wore your glasses

THAT see only Love?

Remember the 1960s Film __Pollyanna__ with Hayley Mills? The young Pollyanna taught the whole town something she called The Glad Game. It goes like this: you take any situation, and find what you could be glad about in it. I love how much we mention Pollyanna. However, it's usually in the negatively cautious context:

"Well, you Don't need to be a Pollyanna about it."

Of course, we Don't need to be mindlessly searching for the positive.

it's also good to be flattened by pain...

WHAT ABOUT MINDFULLY SEARCHING for it, and More important, Allowing it?

It is GOOD to keep A JOURNAL or notes About pleasure. THAT WAY, you will retain or strengthen your pleasure perspective. This involves noticing Joy In tiny places and MAGNifying it.

Here Are some of My recent notes.

A
trio
of
white
butterflies
Dancing
in
THE
sun

COMBING
and
Kissing
My
CAT
Jupiter

listening
To My
Brother
on My
voicemail
say
THAT He
loves Me

PLAYing
ZyDeco
Music
From
New orleans
As I CHange
THe sHeeTs

WHAT BRINGS YOU PLEASURE?

reminders
of
pleasure

WHAT pleasure DO you BrinG?

circle of pleasure

The more pleasure we can learn
to experience, the more we can bring to
others.

Here are some of my recent pleasure
bringings:

complimenting
a woman in my
corner store, telling
her she smelled good.
when I asked her
what it was, she
smiled radiantly
and said
"it's called _angel_"

Giving my
two friends
thick white
robes to
wear
while using
my hot tub

leaving a note
for my neighbor,
appreciating
the paint job
on her building

sending
flowers to
my brother
on his
first day
of teaching
high school

Your pleasure Book

You could begin to keep a journal of all the pleasure in your life

it could be stuffed full of drawings, clippings, photographs, letters, food stains, marks from your teacups, and places for secret notes.

it could also be spare, and simple and randomly opened. You don't need to do it everyday!

You could start and never finish!

You deserve pleasure and

pleasure loves your company!

Measuring Pleasure

Pleasure doesn't just come in slabs or chunks or big thick increments of time.

It also arrives in hints and whispers and slow installments.

Pleasure peeks in and puts a puff of positive... in your pocket!

Sometimes I abandon something before the pleasure even has a chance to get there! At a social gathering, I might judge the people or event itself so quickly that I end up missing the pleasure. So often, I leave a party and find out that the "real party" happened after I left!

I think that pleasure responds to invitation more than declaration.

I can remember Times when my
Attitude was, "where's The pleAsure?" to
such a degree, THAT pleAsure probably
snuck out the BACK Door...

I offer These reminders:

@ let pleAsure Discover you.

@ put yourself in new situations
   and Be pATient.

@ Be open For unexpected pleAsures.

People's PArade of pleAsure

@ AWAken to pleAsure.

@ CreAte invitAtions for pleAsure.

@ WAit for pleAsure to AppeAr.

@ invent scenarios for pleasure
To Appear in, and set the stage.

@ Become the pleasure THAT you
SAY you're seeking. instead
of looking outside, Find THE
pleasure inside your self.

it's THere.

Become THe pleAsure

We can Be our own Dance pArtner

PLEASURE of CHANGING

LATE ONE NIGHT, I WALKED THE LABYRINTH AT GRACE CATHEDRAL IN SAN FRANCISCO. I DEDICATED MY WALK TO "MAKING FRIENDS WITH CHANGE," AND CRIED THE WHOLE TIME.

VERY LOOSE DRAWING OF A LABYRINTH. READ WALKING A SACRED PATH BY Dr. LAUREN ARTRESS

I CRIED BECAUSE I'D BEEN RUNNING AROUND, TRYING TO "KEEP ALL THE LIDS" ON CHANGE. OF COURSE, IT DOESN'T WORK, AND NEW CHANGES WERE DEVELOPING ALL THE TIME!

NO MATTER HOW HARD i TRIED WITH THE LIDS STUFF KEPT BUBBLING OUT...

I SPENT MY ENERGY JUSTIFYING, EXPLAINING, COMPLAINING ABOUT OR JUST AVOIDING THE CHANGES THAT I WAS EXPERIENCING. I REALLY BEGAN TO SEE HOW AVIDLY I WAS TRYING TO KEEP EVERYTHING THE SAME.

It seemed like if I could just keep enough things the same, then I wouldn't have to change my self, or my views, perspectives, attitudes or beliefs.

This rigidity was preventing me from experiencing the pleasures of change. Perhaps the more I could accept and welcome change, the more I myself could change.

CHANGES swirled around me, often while sleeping

WHAT if all my resistance to changing was a kind of arrogance about the movements of the universe?

THAT if I distrust change, then I am in effect distrusting the universe!

I cling so hard to all of my little systems and processes. I find such pleasure in my routines. I am bound by my ideas of time and life.

I want to declare my life to be one big experiment! I want to relish and welcome change, seek out change and find the pleasure in that. I want to be a gifted quick change artist.

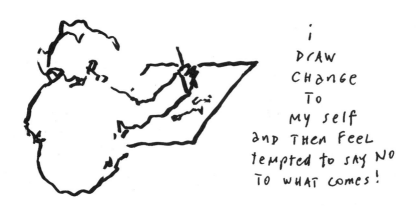

i
draw
change
to
my self
and then feel
tempted to say no
to what comes!

I want to be able to find the safety within the changes, or change my ideas about safety!

Here is my letter to change:

Dear Change,

I've previously been very afraid of you. You weren't welcome in my home, and I spoke badly about you behind your back. I resisted you, avoided you, and made fun of you.

I want to change our relationship. I want to learn to cultivate and respect you, dance with you and take you out to dinner.

Let's travel together!

Will you be my everlasting friend?

Love, Susan

I anticipate experiencing these
pleasures through changing:

Hearing news of others' changes with
great interest and enthusiasm

Noticing myself changing with
openness and self compassion

experiencing change as a neutral
entity, neither "good" nor "bad"

relaxing into change

welcoming and cultivating
change easily

Allowing change to flow
through me

Designing my life with change in mind

receiving the benefits of change

CHanges swirled Happily Around

CHAPTER One · Books + Quotes + Web Sights
Permission for Pleasure

"The Moment of Change is the only Poem"
Adrienne Rich

Phenomenal <u>Woman</u> by Maya Angelou

Paintings by Paul Gauguin

<u>The Artist's Way</u>
<u>Creativity Kit</u>   by Julia Cameron

<u>Moonlight Chronicles</u>   by Dan Price
A Wandering Artist's Journal

<u>How Much Joy Can you Stand</u>?
                    by Suzanne Falter-Barnes

<u>The Vagina Monologues</u>   by Eve Ensler

WeB Sights:
WWW. Moonlightchronicles.com
WWW. HowMuchJoy.com
WWW. VaginaMonologues.com

" A Bird Does not sing Because it Has
an answer— it sings Because it Has A Song"
                    Chinese Proverb

Pleasure in Giving and receiving

Most of us Are very good at giving. There is a lot of pleasure involved with giving, and when we do it, we usually feel good.

Giving creates a bond, an exchange and an opportunity to be generous. Pleasure in giving stops when we do it compulsively, with obligation or in order to "get something" in return.

There is room for growth in the Art of giving and receiving.

The seeds of new ways of giving

Here is a recent story about how I learned something new about receiving.

I was on my book tour and in Washington D.C. to do the radio show, NPR. My limousine driver was named Muhammed, and he had heard my interview on the radio and said he'd felt very moved by what I'd said. Muhammed then declared,

"You are very gifted and I really wish to serve you today."

I explained that he was serving me by driving, and asked him to take me to a park. I got my tennis shoes out of the trunk, and Muhammed ran over and said,

"Please allow me to tie your tennis shoes"

He dropped to his knees before I could even answer. As he tied my shoes, tears came to my eyes as I remembered that the last person to tie them had been my dad.

I am embarrassed to admit that I then noticed that he wasn't tying them very well! They were loose, and the shoelaces were too long. I suddenly realized that I felt extremely uncomfortable at receiving his help, and had to find fault with it in some way.

So I practiced receiving by going on my walk without adjusting the laces, and smiling as they flopped around.

Here Are some questions for you...

Are you Able to Give without any "credit"? Describe

Do you Feel Compelled to Give in Honor of certAin occasions even if you Dont want To? wHen and How

Do you seArch For wAys and reAsons To Give? List some Here

is Giving eAsy For you? shAre A couple of exAmples

no More OBLiGATion presents!

insteAD, Give presence

MORE ABOUT GIVING... PLEASE DESCRIBE:

@ IN WHAT WAYS DO you FEEL SATISFIED OR DISSATISFIED WITH HOW OTHERS GIVE TO YOU?

@ WAYS IN WHICH you WELCOME AND FULLY EMBRACE GIFTS, OR NOT?

@ SHARE A STORY OF A FAVORITE TIME YOU GAVE TO SOMEONE

@ WHAT YOU CAN OFFER TO THE WORLD WITH YOUR GIVING?

SOME QUESTIONS FOR YOU ABOUT RECEIVING...

@ TELL ABOUT A FAVORITE TIME THAT SOMEONE GAVE TO YOU

@ DESCRIBE WAYS THAT RECEIVING MAKES YOU UNCOMFORTABLE

@ TELL ABOUT YOUR STYLE OF RECEIVING

@ WHAT ARE SOME WAYS YOU COULD EXPAND YOUR ABILITY TO RECEIVE?

I AM FASCINATED BY THE SUBJECT of receiving. Most people Aren't very GOOD AT it, and the <u>worst</u> <u>receivers</u> <u>Are</u> <u>usually</u> <u>The</u> <u>Best</u> <u>Givers.</u>

As A novice receiver, I've Been studying THe subject For A WHILE, and notice How often and effectively I "Block" receiving.

WHy is THis? I think it's Because I Feel out of control and vulnerABle WHen I receive, and some pArt of Me is MeAsuring and counting WHether it is "FAir" or "equAl."

SAD little ScoreBoard

"let's see... it's proBABly not FAir to Ask Her To Drive Me, I Didn't respond To Her lAst request..."

& retire THe "counter!"

AT THe BottoM of All this is A Me THAT Feels <u>unworthy</u> of receiving.

So I turn and rush away to try
to cover up the shame I feel at my
inability to really receive. Or, I falsely
give, to regain some sense of "control."

When I'm giving,
I feel powerful,
good, and that
I'm "doing the
right thing."

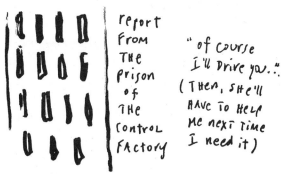

report
from
the
prison
of
the
control
factory

"of course
I'll drive you.":
(then, she'll
have to help
me next time
I need it)

I've begun experimenting
with asking for and receiving help from
others. I've also begun asking other people
how often or well they ask for help.

The resounding answers have been:

"never!"

"only if I really have to"

"I don't want to be a burden
or owe anyone"

"I'm pretty independent"

"Very rarely, and only for the
best reasons"

"only if I can give something back"

"Oh no. I don't like asking for help"

"I don't like feeling dependent
on anyone"

let's explore my latest receiving lesson:
I think I'm brought to my best lessons
by some kind of darkness. in this
particular darkness, I was exhausted,
flattened by travel and work, and
needed to leave the next day for more work.

   I felt like one of those cartoon
characters that gets flattened and
then gradually regains its shape,
only I was still staying flat.

   I woke
up the
next day

crushed, squished and flattened by life

feeling frustrated,
lonely and overwhelmed.

I prepared to endure those emotions
as I have so many times before, and
as tears dotted my pillow,
a little voice said,

"You could ask for some help"

Teary Pillow

I put the pillow over my head.

Then I picked up the phone and called
my life coach, Patricia. During our phone
session, I investigated my current state,
changed my misperceptions, released shame,
allowed my actual experience, brought
light into my necessary darkness, and
I laughed heartily at my humanity
and splendid imperfections.

By the end of our talk, I felt ready
to call for some help, and noticed my
relief and gladness as I surrendered
to it. I made 2 calls for some help,
and watched myself nervously chatter
i just love voicemail, don't you?
on their phone messages as I tried to
"make it okay" to receive the help.

WHile WAITing for responses To MY cAlls for HeLp, I BeGan My work of releAsing My expectations THAT HeLp WOULD Be AVAilABle.

As it turned out, BoTH Friends were ABle and willing To HeLp, and I oBserved How MVcH I tried to JusTiFy needing THe HeLp, anyThing But Just GrAciously Accept it!

I reALized THAT I'm AFrAid THAT people won't tell The TruTH ABout whether THey're ACTVALly AVAilABle To HeLp. I FeAr They'll AGree (out of oBLiGATion, pressure or "people pleAsing"), and THen Arrive with some undercurrent of Bitterness.

HAD I Done THis too? I THink so. I'M Also AFrAid of My requesT Being reJecteD, and THen TAKing it personAlly! So, I'D rATHer Just skip it and

HOW DARE THEY NOT HELP ME!

DO eVeryTHinG MYSelf

This is where true isolation and feelings of unworthiness come in.

I want to learn the pleasures of conscious giving and receiving. When we consciously receive, we give another the

(Opportunity To Be Generous.)

receiving is a gift to the giver.

if we cannot receive, then we cannot truly give.

I want to gloriously and graciously receive, without count or measure.

I want to lose track of "who gave" and "who received".

I want to eagerly do both, with truth and integrity.

I want to have patience with all of my stumblings along the way.

There are so many places to trip and stumble

new perspectives

My friend PATRICIA SHARED with me that after her life-threatening illness, she still couldn't receive. She sat with her shaved head, in a darkened house, with no groceries. It was only then that she finally turned to someone to receive help.

receiving is a strength, not a weakness

So many of us were emotionally abandoned as children, and learned that the only safety or thing to count on, was:

DOING IT ALL BY OURSELVES

Our pride puffs up, and we use it to try and fill the emptiness, to feel "beholden to no one."

I offer a new look at all of this: The possibility of

pure pleasure
AT
giving and receiving

pride
loves
to
puff up

Let us:

circles of HELP

- @ FORM HELPING circles

- @ TALK ABOUT GiVing aud receiving with Friends, aud estABLiSH HeALThy BoundAvies

- @ Tell THe TrvTH ABout WHAT We're willing To GiVe or receive

- @ upDATe THAT List often

- @ Become Skilled AT receivimg

- @ Become DifferenTly Skilled AT Giving

WE ARE WorTHy, I Know THis now.

receiving note: of Course there Are The TAKers, THe MoocHes, THe CHeATers, THe MALingerers. We Know THis too... it's o.K.

WE Are WorTHY

CHAPTER TWO · BOOKS + QUOTES + WEB SIGHTS
GIVING and RECEIVING

" THE HEALTHY, the STRONG iNDIVIDUAL is THE one
WHO ASKS for HELP WHEN He needs it — whether
He's Got an ABCESS on His KNEE or in His SOUL "
RONA BARRETT

HOW you DO anyTHING is HOW you DO everyTHING
BY CHERi HUBER

Seven WONDERS: everyDAY THINGS for A
HEALThier planet
BY JOHN C. RYan

You can HEAL your Life
BY LOUISE HAY

CALM Surrender
BY Kent NERBURN

Bone: Dying into Life
BY MARion WOODMan

WEB SIGHTS:
WWW. for the little ones inside.com
WWW. HAYHOUSE.com
WWW. comfort Queen. com

" NO AMOunt of Self· improvement Can MAKE
up for A lack of Self. Acceptance "
ROBERT HOLDEN

ADDING People To Your PleAsure

I AM an introvert, and I enjoy Doing Things Alone, and Being Alone. Sometimes my Aloneness is A WAY To Avoid people and How out of control I often Feel with Them.

I Actually Forget About the joy That people can Bring. My own mind can Feel very SMALL, my own Activities Limited, and I Begin To wish For the TUMULT and unpredictABiLity of other people.

As I write This, I wonder How many other people Feel Like I Do.

Sometimes it seems To Me THAT other people "GET TOGETHer" eAsily and naturally, and THAT I'm The only UnComForTABLe,

TUMULT and unpredictAbility
of
P e o p l e

Highly sensitive, wishing-I-was-home-in-bed person. Then as I continue to share my life process in my books, I continue to find myself surrounded by other like-minded souls. lots of them.

even if someone doesnt share my particular experience, perhaps he/she can better understand people like me!

Here are some things I find pleasurable about other people:

· They are not me!
this may seem obvious. but I forget

· They say or do things that can truly surprise + delight me
this often happens

· Their humanity can touch and awaken mine

People are very poignant

Kindred spirits

50

I Find it interesting How often I Forget The wonders THAT other people Bring, and The Alchemy THAT's created.

recently I'd Been SAD and Depressed, and Feeling isolated. "reAching out" To someone seemed Like an extremely Difficult task.

Then I remembered THAT I'd MADE A plan With Friends for 8 o'clock THAT night. I immediately THOUGHT ABout CHangiNG or canceling The plan, But Then Decided To keep it, in Hopes of Finding some pleasure.

2,000 pound phone

THeir BeAming FAces Melted Me

THank you roBin and John!

As soon as I saw my Friends' BeAming FAces, some Frozen part of me Melted,

and we swirled away into the night
for grilled artichokes, good red wine
and uproarious conversation. Later
we sat by candlelight, sharing the
revelations and puzzles of our lives.
   When my friends
left at 4 a.m., I
truly felt replenished.
   The pleasure of the
evening had added
dimension to my
earlier depression.
   It was important
that I experienced the
depression, and it was
equally important that I
step out of it and refresh my spirit.

we must refresh our spirits

   There is such magic and
mystery about how people affect us.
   I was at my dry cleaners, and
saw a man standing at the counter

52

With His BACK to Me, weAring A
BeAutiFuL purple sHirt.
  I SAid, "GreAT purple SHirt!"
He turned slowly Around with A
GreAT smile, and sAid,
  "your smile looks JusT Like
  Goin' in THe cookie JAr!"
  I Grinned All THe wAy Home, and
THe Memory still MAkes Me smile.
  in new york city on My Book tour,
I cAlled My Friend Bill to see if
He wanted to "Go out and plAy." He
DiD, and BrovGHT AlonG A BuckeT
of BriGHTly colored CHALK.

BiG
Colored
CHALK

H U G e
B i G
B U C k e T
of
C H A L K

After Dinner we took A Horse
and Carriage ride to central park,
pretending to be visitors with
Different names. i think I was natasha...

We Found A perfect spot to
Begin coloring with CHALK, and
By lamplight, we sketched and
Laughed, and wrote Messages
and Affirmations for people
To Find.

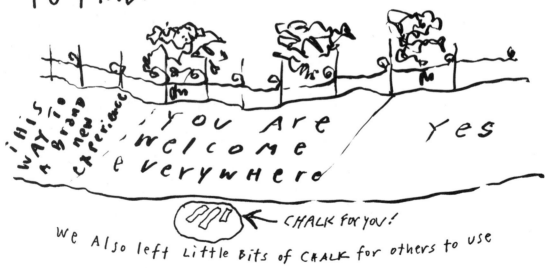

this is way to A Brand new experience

You Are welcome everywhere   yes

← CHALK For you!

we Also left little bits of CHALK for others to use

As we left The PArK, we Turned
To see where we HAD entered,

and there, etched into the stone wall were these words:

ARTIST'S GATE

So we colored these too!

I went BACK THE next DAY TO
see All the Art and words THAT
people HAD ADDed ÷ it WAS THrilling
To see!

People HAD ADDed on THeir own messAGes

STory of THE serendipitous HAircut
Often while writing A BOOK, I
Become isolAted and rATHer perAnged,
even THOUGH I know thAt seeing people
COULD Heup. On THis pArticular DAY, My
HAir WAs in My eyes and I Felt rATHer
Desperate For A HAircut. Does HAir weAr A Dress?
I cAlled My DeAr HAir Dresser BiBBO,
and Asked if He WOULD Be willing to
MAke A HOUse cAll. (I Felt Very nervous Asking THis)
"Of course Gorgeous! AnyTHing for you,"
He replied.

BiBBo Arrived with A Bouquet of pink-
and-white zinnias and A Beaming smile.
He shared stories of transformations
and mythology, and reminded me of
my purpose.
      I sent out requests for support on
e-mail, and this is what my agents
wrote BACK:

dearest, i can only imagine what it must be like!
whenever i think of you in the creation process of a new book, i always
envision you in a magical cocoon...then, at the end, this big, amazing,
technicolor butterfly breaks free and astounds both the world and itself. so
just know we're here, ever so aware of you "in there," patiently awaiting
your emergence with love!
  if that imagery doesn't help, try Snackwells. They work every time.

                            THank you D!

well I don't blame you! 120 pages is FABULOUS. how is it all going in
your splendid isolation? Please remember that I stand by ready to read
anything and everything if it would be at all helpful. I think this new book
is going to be wonderful!
                            THank you M!

      One night, After A Friend HAD Called
To say she couldnt get Together, I
knew I still needed some Company,
so I went out in search of some.

AT THESE TIMES, I PAY close Attention
To the energy and Movements of other
people, wondering if THEY MIGHT Be MY
new Friends.

I noticed A
lovely couple AT
THe Top of some
STAirs near My
Home. We traded
Smiles and stories
of steep Hills.
THeresA and Mike
were visiting From
NORTH CAROLINA.

BOTH GiFTed Artists and HuMan Beans

I invited them To join Me on MY WALK
and THey enthusiastically Agreed. AFTer
WATCHing THe sunset, we went To Dinner
ToGether. We Were Definitely Kindred
Spirits who shared spontaneous pleAsure
toGether.

WE can TrUST serenDiPity

It still surprises me every time how CLOSE people actually are. During times of isolation, being connected with others seems utterly hopeless. Then, within moments, I can be experiencing the pleasure of other people and their energy.

Children really know this. When children get together, they dont know what they'll "do" and they dont care!

They get together for a sort of human communion

I want to remember this. I want to keep this very fresh in my mind when a friend calls to "get together."

There is such pleasure in the radiantly simple moments:

easy
company
of kids

- Conversations over TeA
- Desserts with 2 spoons
- lost in The CAR, LAUGHING
- SMuGGLiNG Food inTo The Movie Theater
- TALKiNG on The phone About everything + nothing

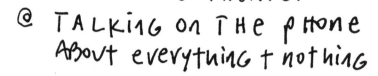

The phrase "The pleAsure of your company" is A Truly lovely one.

Let's remember and Treaswe The pleAsure THAT other people Bring us!

nourishing words and LAughTer

CHApTer THree. BOOKS + Quotes + WeB SiGHTS
ADDiNG people To your pleAsure

" We Are DANciNG THrovGH eACH oTHer AS
DoorwAyS. we Are ripples crossing aud FUSiNG,
Journeying aud returniNG" MArGe piercy

THe BiG O OrGASMS: By Lou pAGeT
HOW To HAve THem, Give THem and keep THem comiNG

STArGirL   By Jerry Spinelli

Trusting Soul   By Brian audreAS

The persistence of yellow:
Book of recipes for Life   By MoNique DuvAL
                    illvstrations By JoanNA ABBott Moss

TAke Time for your LiFe
                By CHeryL richArdson

WeB SiGHTS:
www. storypeople. com
www. Freewill AstroloGy. com
www. BArBrA sHer. com

" CourAGe is very importaNt. Like A Mvscle,
  it is strengTheNed By Use "
                    ruTh GorDoN

Pleasure no Matter WHAT!

OH, How we cling To the "GOOD" experiences and Turn AWAY From THE "BAD" ones. During My LAST BOOK tour, I HAD WHAT COULD Be Described As A Beatific DAY.

The DAY Began in A 4-poster FEATHER BED, Top and Bottom! and proceeded To an 8-Foot-long CLAW-Foot BATHtub.

THiCK puffy Down
I could See the Glorious TUB From My BED

I WAS THEN TAKEN TO AN OLD VICTORIAN HOUSE FOR A MASSAGE, AND AS I STEPPED OUT OF THE CAR, THE GARDENER SAW ME AND SAID, "WAIT!"

SHE FLUNG FLOWER PETALS ONTO THE GROUND FOR ME TO WALK UPON!

MY MASSAGE TOOK PLACE IN A TREEHOUSE WITH THE SCENT OF LAVENDER AND THE SOUND OF BIRDS.

THAT NIGHT I THOUGHT, "AHA! THIS IS FINALLY THE euphoric LIFE OF PLEASURE THAT I DESERVE.

ALL I SAW OUT THE WINDOW WERE BRANCHES + BIRDS

I SHALL HAVE MORE TOMORROW."

let's JUST see...

WHEN I WOKE UP THE NEXT DAY,
THE FIRST THING I noticed WAS A THROBBING
HEADACHE THAT CAME From GriADing MY
TeeTH in MY sleep. NeXT, I noticed it
WAS CHilly in THe room, aND raiNY
outside.   O H   i S H

    SUDDenly I FeLT so Homesick THAT
I BeGan To cry. WHen I looKed Ai THe
DAY'S scHeDule, it All FeLT LiKe too MUCH,
aND no FUN AT All.   no FuN

WHere HAD All the pleAsure Gone?
    it seeMed to Me THAT All the
pleAswes of THe DAY BeForc HAD
          V a n i s H e D
    I FeLT sullen auD Dull, auD very
un williNG To FiND any pleAswe AT All.

it seeMed to Me THAT THere
WAS JUST A SMAll puDDle
WHere pleAsure HAD Been

Then I remembered.

There was pleasure to be found in the midst of my sullen mood too.

I just had to look a little harder, and narrow my focus a bit. If I could (Accept) my headache, and the rain, and the feeling of homesickness, what else might develop?

As soon as I had this thought, there was a knock at the door, and it was the owner of the inn;

"I thought you might like a pot of hot tea and some scones that I just baked."

I did, and my mood shifted a bit.

The day contained other challenges: missed appointments, a late taxi, a "bad" seat on an airplane, and a hotel room right next to a loud elevator...

They serve breakfast by candlelight!

Awesome scone ↓

Thank you to Lanning + Steve owners of the White House in Portland Oregon

65

How we view these incidents in our lives, and how well we can contain our actual experiences (instead of the experiences we wish for or prefer) can enable us to multiply the pleasures within them.

$$2 \times 4 = 8$$

and actually, the multiplication increases according to perception of received pleasure!

Here are some unlikely places I've found pleasure and what I did to discover or create it.

elevator next to hotel room:
every time I heard the distinctive "ding" of the elevator, I used it to check and see if I was actually in the present moment, and to use it as a reminder to do so.
I was only in the present moment
 twice in 2 days!

At the periodontist:
I named my periodontist "Demon rose" (she liked to tell jokes, and since she sometimes inflicted pain, I named her Demon rose, which we endlessly laughed about)
 I also brought in special music to create an alternate environment. sometimes I stopped treatment to ask for a hug.

The Bank: Thanks to Dave!

I gave copies of my books to the manager, and he keeps them on a shelf by his desk, and lets people borrow them.

I like to share kind words, unusual comments, or laughter with the tellers.

Sometimes I do little drawings for them.

If you offer pleasure, you usually receive pleasure.

Finding pleasure <u>no matter what</u> is an art to be practiced.

THE
ART
of finding
PLEASURE
everywhere

we can use new tools and perspectives

If you are used to <u>reacting</u> badly when bad things happen, you will need some time to shift perspective.

Here are some imaginary scenarios to practice finding pleasure in:

How can you imagine relating
Differently to each of these situations?

Your car
is towed

Usual response:

Unusual response:
where's the pleasure?

You Didn't
Get a loan,
or Financial
Aid

Usual response:

Unusual response:

It is so easy to just get MAD,
take it out on other people and refuse
to find any pleasure at all.

This is especially tempting when
there has been an injustice, or a mistake
made.

it DOESN'T MEAN YOU CAN'T GET

reAlly MAD

it DOES MEAN YOU CAN GO BEYOND it...

let's Keep prACticing

or not. your CHOICE!
note: iMAGINING an exercise
is often As powerfull As DOING it

THE Dry cleaner lost your Clothes, Airlines lost your BAGS

USUAL response:

UNUSUAL response:

your credit report is Full of inAccurAcies

USUAL response:

UNUSUAL response:

I Always THink of GerALD JAMPOLSKY, WHo wrote Love is letting GO of FEAr and said, "WOULD YOU RATHER BE RIGHT, or HAVE PEACE of MIND?" I wanted BOTH

For so many years, I would rather be right, and my life showed it. I was frequently MAD AT SOMETHING, and my pleasure disappeared or was diminished in the face of my "problems".

pleasure crushed by weight of problems

Then I realized that the problems were being magnified by (ME), and that I was actually trying to find pleasure in that!

So, I found my "pleasure" in
- COMPLAINING
- DETAILING INJUSTICES
- repetitive negative stories
- pointing out the "better way"
- finding others to be at fault

So Many experiences in our lives Are NOT THOUGHT of As pleasurable. Since we spend so much time dealing with Them, let's learn to Find The pleasures within Them!

We can learn to change, surrender, and let go of looking good or being right.

It Also involves putting an emphasis on The pleasure within The pain, and creating experiences THAT Are new and Joy·Full.

Can you Find The word pleasure Hidden in This scene? of course you can! Pleasure is Always near...

I now concentrate on Finding The pleasure inside the pain. It's Always* There, and even if you can't locate it, Take pleasure in HAVing Tried!

* O.K., O.K., it's usually There

Pleasure During Difficult Times

While I was writing this book, my mother was very ill, and in and out of the hospital in Minnesota. As I attempted to assist from a distance, and remain poised to go there, I watched myself retreat into a cave of depression. I stopped doing pleasurable things.

I thought that somehow it honored my mother's pain to deny myself pleasure. I had also stopped exercising and eating nutritious foods. My eating disorder was reactivated, and I developed what felt like agoraphobia: fear of going out or being with people.

The eye of the cave

Meanwhile, this book on (pleasure) was due.

pleasure of what?

HOW COULD I Write About pleAsure if
I WASn't Able To HAve any? In My
isolated state, pleasure Felt impossible
To Attain, and very FAr AWAY.

Then I reAlized THAT THis is exactly
WHAT I MUST Write About: My process of
Accepting and creating pleasure During
really Difficult Times.

WHAT I've noticed is THAT pleAsure
MiGHT recede, But it's AlwAys closer
THan we Think.

I BeGan CULTivATinG
MUCH Tinier pleAsures
DUring THis TIme.
I MArveleD AT
perfectly sTeAMeD
BroccoLi, THe curleD
edGes of My new canDle,
rAinBow colored DUst Motes.

eeny
Teeny
Tiny
pleAsures

My usual pleasures MiGHT HAve TemporArily
sTopped, But if I JUST nArrowed My vision
and SHiFTeD My perspective, I couLD locAte
Tiny pleAsures!

We can find gentle humor in the most terrible circumstances and tenderness in the darkness.

We're all tender little beans, bouncing along

Joy and pleasure are not reserved for when "things are good". They can be our solace when things are not good at all.

I spent time with my mom while she was sick and treasured our tiny pleasures of eating grilled cheese sandwiches and watching old movies together. When it was time for me to leave, I felt very sad and tried to cover it up with false cheer.

My mom has a square little pan. Just for grilled cheese

"See you soon!" I smiled brightly

"Feel better!" I called out happily

"I'll call you when I get home!" I promised cheerily

False cheer masks flew off

WHAT I ACTUALLY FELT WAS TREMENDOUS FEAR AND SADNESS THAT I MIGHT NOT SEE HER AGAIN.

I GOT INTO THE WAITING TAXI, AND AS IT PULLED AWAY, I BEGAN TO CRY. THESE WERE NOT QUIET TEARS, BUT GULPING, MESSY, SOBBING TEARS, AND I FELT VERY EMBARRASSED TO BE CRYING LIKE THIS IN PUBLIC, IN FRONT OF THIS CAB DRIVER. I COULDN'T STOP CRYING, AND I WONDERED WHAT HE MUST BE THINKING. THEN, WHEN HE PULLED THE CAB OVER TO THE SIDE OF THE ROAD, I THOUGHT,

"HE'S GOING TO ASK ME TO GET OUT!"

HE TURNED TO LOOK AT ME WITH KIND EYES AND SAID,

"THANK GOD FOR YOUR TEARS! I BLESS YOUR TEARS! I AM SO HONORED TO BE IN THIS CAR WITH YOU AND YOUR TEARS."

HE ASKED WHY I WAS CRYING, AND I TOLD HIM.

SYMPHONY
OF
TEARS

He told me that he was from Nigeria, and that his mother had died last year.

"I remember this pain, and I want to remind you that it is GREAT LOVE THAT is bringing you this pain. Your MOMMY will Die. MAYBe TODAY, or next year, we do not know. WHAT we DO know is THAT you MUST Live Deeply All of your precious Moments."

We Drove on, and He told Me About His MOTHer's DEATH, and His Trip BACK TO THE Village in nigeriA. I Cried HARDer, and THen He pulled THe CAB over AGAin, and we Cried TOGETHer.

By THe TiMe I GOT TO THe Airport, I FeLT weAk and LiMp From Crying, yet AT peAce, and Fully in My BODy.

i FeLT STronGer From THe TeArs

THis wAS My pleAsure in THe MiDST of My pAin.

Joy and pleasure really can be our escorts through painful times if we let them in.

We need to realize the necessity of pleasure, not the luxury of it.

Our spirits need pleasure, like our bodies need vitamins, oxygen or water.

Allow pleasure (in) to help heal you and others.

vitamin P

Pleasure in doing Things Badly

My friend rebecca Latimer, in Her book You're not old until you're ninety, speaks beautifully about This:

"Meditation works even when you do it Badly, so dont wait until you're 'Better.' Just start now. This Also applies To everything else."

I'M A recovering perfectionist and its very difficult for me To release my self-expectations, and do "less Than My Best."
So when I was at The Dentist's recently, I made a bold move. The Hygienist was digging around in The plaque in my teeth, and it was so hot in the room, sweat was trickling into My ears!

Do your best
Always say Thank you
Be on Time
Be nice
Always always
Crushed By The Sheer Weight of self-expectations

I put my hand on her arm, and said, "We'll stop here"
   She replied,
   "But we're not done!"
   I told her it was O.K. to do it badly or partially, and unclipped my little dental bib, thanked her, told her I'd return for more another day and LEFT.

That little dental bib...

   I felt such new, sheer pleasure at leaving before it was perfect.

   I'm learning to just show up and do what I can, even when it's not up to my "usual standards". I'm going to learn how to have lots of standards!

   I bought this book about perfection, and the title haunted me every time I saw it.

never good enough by Monica Ramirez Basco Ph.D.

excellent book, by the way

SO, I took THE JACKET off THE BOOK
and wrote Directly onto THE HARDCOVER

G O O D

e n o U G H

THese words Bring Me pleAsure
every Time I see THEM, and remind Me
THAT I can Be

V A r i A B l e   and

F l A W e D

and even Do some THings
BADly!

WHAT
if
I GAVe
A
Dinner
PARTy
and
noBopy
CAMe?

i COULD MonopoLize THe ConversATion...

So Here Are some THings I Do/HAve Done "BADly:"

My editor SAiD I WAS Being Too HArD on Myself... Not For A Perfectionist!

- SAying yes WHen I Mean no
- Agreeing To Do THings without Full understanding
- not completing My will
- AVoiDing DeNTAL/MeDICAL Appointments
  (resulting in pAinFuL aND expensive TreATMents)
- resisting Going To WeDDings
- Flossing too Briefly
- not recycling everyTHing, or ever enough!
- not DeFrosting My Freezers
  (one Freezer is ToTally Frozen sHut and unusABLe)
- AVoiDing Going To Self-serve GAs stations
  (spending More AT Full-serve)

You GeT THe idea. now My plan is To GeT More pleAsure out of Doing More THings BADly.

Here's A list:
- Doing More pAintings THAT Don't "turn out"
- inferior yoGA and pilAtes prActice
- HAving A Dinner pArty

I GeT So SCAreD To FAiL

81

- Meditation retreats that scare me, and giving myself permission to leave before they're over
- Wilderness hiking
- Being bisexual and going on a date or a heterosexual one!
- Making more health-care appointments and changing them as needed

Proceed Anyway

I think we can open up and do more badly, poorly, incompetently, and find pleasure there too.

I play the piano every day in an amateur fashion, and yet receive so much pleasure from it. I know that my pleasure could drain away if I tried to become a "skilled pianist."

MY HAPPY Piano

i compose sounds that please me

My yoga practice is wobbly and self-styled, and I really enjoy it.

Of course there's room for expertise, competence and "Being our best."

There's a lot more room for playing in other realms, too.

Take pleasure in:
· A poorly planned picnic
· an ill-conceived car trip
· A rainy baseball game
· Feeble hiking

What experiments can you make with "accomplishments" in your life?

What can you do BADLY and more OFTEN?

GOOD YOGA BOOK ↓

Open BODY
BY TODD WALTON
DRAWINGS BY VANCE LAWRY

Pleasure in DRAMA, STress, overwork

Remember THAT THere can Be pleasure in suffering. We sometimes create scenarios of DRAMA, STress or overwork To Fill WHAT Feels Like empty places in ourselves.

I see people TreAT work As "THe enemy" and Forget THAT THeir own THOUGHT processes Are contriButing To THeir DispleAsure. THey Are certAin THAT work is THe problem and if only THey coulD JUST Be AT Home, or not working, THeya Be HAPPy.

WHAT people MIGHT not reAlize is THAT Being AT Home, especiAlly working AT HOME, is A plAyground for unDisciplined THoughts and another kind of stress.

it's usually very Busy... I CAUGHT it AT A quiet Moment

PlAYground of unDisciplined THoughts

It can be very tempting to create DRAMA and escape from feeling ordinary. It is very pleasant to have a DRAMATIC story to tell, and have the focus on (Y O U.)

Stress is another acceptable outlet for escaping. People can claim "stress" and get out of taking responsibility for many things. Overwork is another convenient trap. The ego loves to think we are so important that we must work (really hard) and (A lot) and therefore, we are (very important) which feels pleasurable...

To the ego
remember to look at the origins of pleasure and what you do to create it.

This Person...

WHAT will be written in your book of pleasure?

experiment with Defining your life in
Different ways and realize THAT DRAMA,
stress and overwork Are All choices,
and not something THAT JUST HAppeus To you.
YOU actually HAppen To eAch of THose
stAtes of BeinG.

Begin To Find and create pleasure in
new ways and places. FAmiliN pleasures Are
not Always The Most nourishing choices.

review THe subject of pleAsure in
your life and see if THere Are stAle,
stAGnant or repetitive plAces you GO To
FinD pleAsure THAT Arent truly pleasurABle.

new plAces for pleAsure To plAy

Try This:

Choose Again! when you're feeling tense, overwhelmed, crabby or besieged...

1. let yourself (Be) tense, overwhelmed, crabby and besieged, without judging.

2. see if it's time to give yourself a new attitude and an activity that supports that attitude.

You can keep choosing again as often as you need to.

remember: pleasure can be found tucked into pockets and corners, and exist alongside your work.

Be present for your feelings right now

Then

Choose:

A new attitude

A new activity

Pleasure Alongside Dying

My dear friend Rebecca made a conscious choice to stop eating and die. Her age of 94 and health conditions made it somewhat easier for me to understand her choice, and she asked for my support for her decision.

I made several trips to be with Rebecca, and listened to her resolve as she spoke about her choice to die. I watched myself change and my resistance slip away as I honored her life, and now her death. I felt such pleasure sitting on her bed, just holding her hand. We communicated without

The pleasure of her dying company

words and I could clearly feel our
souls speaking. In those moments, I
thought of what Ram Dass had written:
"Death is not an outrage" and it
felt true.

When I left Rebecca's house, the whole
experience had pitched me keenly into the
present moment, and I stood outside,
breathing deeply and crying freely. We
had said good-bye, and it felt full and
safe.

Those precious moments in her dying
company fortified me and convinced me
that dying is awesome and ordinary and
utterly acceptable.

From the Tangle
A Bird Flew Free

When I got home that night, I wrote these words in my journal:

I sat with my friend Rebecca today. She is dying, and an owl has taken up residence in the big tree outside her window. She speaks of being excited to die, and is looking forward to the adventure of it.

The Owl Spirit

"Can you imagine what I'll be seeing?" she said excitedly.

We had had many conversations about this sort of thing, yet it astonished me to witness her living, her dying.

I held her hand and looked into her eyes. We just stared at each other, and it seemed that I could see right into her soul. Her skin is translucent and she appears pink and new, even at 94. I asked if she would come and see me after her death, and she calmly said,

"it will be the first thing that I do."

FURTHER GIFTS OF DEATH

There is a trail near my home that I like to walk at night, with a full moon and no fog. On this night, I was walking alone in honor of my friend Rebecca, who had died that day.

Usually I experience some fear and anxiety along the path, as I hear animal noises and imagine shapes in the darkness. I felt very aware of Rebecca's spirit, and it seemed to me that she was in everything: in the leaves, the rainbow

SHAPES in THE DARKNESS

around the moon, and even the crunching gravel beneath my feet.

I dropped my fear in that instant, and it never returned, as I walked the miles to the ocean, through the woods and back again.

MY PATH WAS CLEAR

I WALKED WITH PRAYERS IN MY HEART AND
FELT FULLY SUPPORTED BY THE EARTH. IT FELT
ASTONISHING TO WALK WITHOUT FEAR.

LATER THAT NIGHT, MY FRIEND REBECCA APPEARED
CLEARLY IN MY DREAM. THIS IS WHAT SHE SAID:

"FIRST OF ALL, TIME IS NOT WHAT
YOU THINK IT IS. WHAT MIGHT SEEM
LIKE 4 SECONDS, COULD ACTUALLY
BE 4 THOUSAND YEARS.

YOU'RE LIVING RIGHT NEXT TO PARALLEL
UNIVERSES, ALL STACKED UP NEXT TO
EACH OTHER.

ALSO, YOU WERE RIGHT. I'M IN EVERYTHING.

I AM NOT THE FORMERLY SOLID
BODY YOU KNEW AS REBECCA.
THERE IS ABSOLUTELY
no need
TO BE SAD"

This Dream visit from Rebecca freed
me from many anxieties I had held
about death, and awakened me to the
possibilities of the

Pleasures of Death.

Rebecca told me she was excited
to die, and I believed her. Clearly
this means that I could also be excited
to take that journey.

I remember my friend Miriam telling
me about her multiple near-death experiences.

"It was so beautiful, I could barely
come back. It felt excruciating to
turn away from that light."

We Are Made of Light

She told me that she had never feared death again.

What I fear is the loss of attachments, terrible pain and the (unknown) oh dear.

It is clear to me that we must live our deaths, and be awake for our dying.

I want to explore all the possibilities that death brings, not just the scary ones.

MAY WE ALL BE BLESSED
WITH CONSCIOUS DEATHS

AND BREATHS

CHAPTER FOUR. BOOKS + QUOTES + WEB SIGHTS
PLEASURE NO MATTER WHAT!

"eternity is not something THAT BEGINS AFTER you Are DEAD. It is Going on All the time. we Are in it now"

CHARLotte PERKINS GILMAN

FINDING A JOYFUL LIFE in the Heart of pAin
BY DArlene CoHen

AWAKENING From Grief   BY JOHN E. WELSHONS

STIll Here   BY RAM DASS

After the ecstasy, THE LAUNDRY
BY JACK KornField

GOD is no LAUGHING MAHer
BY JuliA CAMeron

WEB SIGHT:
WWW. LifeCHAHenGes. OrG

"it's A nice DAY to Go To HeAven"
MoTHer TeresA

95

Tiny Travels
Trips of pleasure inside your Home

Our Homes Are Filled with pleasures
That Are Forgotten, or Hiding, or simply
not seen. We gravitate to the obvious
pleasures, and repeat WHAT HAS BROUGHT
us pleasure Before: the BED, The television,
refrigerator, telephone...

Obvious Home Pleasures

You can Begin to explore The Tinier
realms of pleasure inside your Home.
  Here Are some Things To Try:
1. visiting in your own Home:
    enter your Home AS Though you've
    never Been there Before. Comment
    or exclaim over WHAT you Find lovely
    or unusual. sit in A Different

CHAIR, turn on Different lamps, Use A Dish you never Take out. Look at Books you Haven't seen in Ages. Open them randomly and see what they say to you. Use the phone on your other ear, Dial By letters, not numbers. If you never cook, Bake something. If you Cook, Ask someone over to cook for you.

BOOKS SPEAK SUBLIMELY in Their own language

There is so much pleasure in your Home That you might not have experienced, visit and see!

2. I am one of the Most repetitive Creatures I know, and am continually experimenting with my environment in order to wake up.

Our Homes Are really Just Laboratories for experimentation.

Our little Home laboratories...

97

Here are some things to try:
Write on your walls with multicolored
chalk. (you can always paint it over later)
I just wrote on the wall in my front hall

everybody loves you

in bright fuchsia chalk.

Put your pillows on the other end of
the bed and pull the covers around you
from the end of the bed.

Watch videotapes you've never watched,
and write a poem afterwards.

Borrow music that you've never heard
of from the library.

If you have a computer, my friend
Andrea suggests this: make up words
for a web sight and see what you get!

i entered redbike.com
and got a whole screen
of unreadable letters!
I thought maybe it was
spies...
But it just turned out
that my little netpliance™
couldnt read the program!

I do actually
recommend the
i-opener™, which is
a netyliance™, cheap
way to get on the
internet and send
e mail...
1-800-467-3637

Be upside down in Different corners of your House. Get A plant and Trust Yourself with its cARe.

reAD Poetry loudly in your pAJAMAS with every LIGHT in your House BURNING. THink of new experiments! Use All THE Closets, too.

3. Give AWAY

Set objects Free! They want to get out

CircuLATe THe OBJECTs in your Home. Give THings AWAY Frequently.

eSTABLisH Give AWAY spots in your neiGHBorHooD (I use My lAUNDroMAT).

More experiments!

WALK BACKwArds everywHere

MAke posters or Art THAT Fit over your TV screen. rotATe THem.

Write A L O V e letter To yourself on THe inside of your BATHTUB or sHower WiTH

Bright red Lipstick

Hello Gorgeous!

The happy tub

Thank your toilet.
O.K., I just put that in to see if you were listening, although it wouldn't be a bad idea. it just sounds funny...

So many good things just sound funny! Let's forget about how things sound or look, or whether we'll look "Foolish."

Fun is often FOOLISH!

Take tiny trips of pleasure inside your home and talk about what you see.

It will multiply your pleasure in Living.

Tiny Travels

"MY BED IS WARM, MY PILLOW DEEP,
TODAY'S THE DAY I'M GOING TO SLEEP"
Dr. Seuss

How To Draw A cup of coffee By Joy Sikorski

Promise of Sleep   By William Dement, PH.D.

Prayers for Healing   edited By Maggie Oman

everyone wants to go to Heaven, But...
                              By C. McNair Wilson

The Okay Book   By Todd Parr

WEB SIGHTS:
www.mcnairwilson.com
www.superbad.com

SARK's inspiration Line
"A place to Be How you
Actually Are"
(24 Hours) 415.546.3742 (epic)

"i found God in Myself ; I loved Her... i
loved Her Fiercely"
                          nTozake Shange

I send you... a tiny fairy with
a lantern, flying nearby, to keep you company.
I send you the long stare of a beloved cat, and a
fast ride in a red convertible with the top down.
I send you piano music by candlelight, and a bright,
soft piece of cloth   to wrap yourself in.

I send you honest questions from children, and the
sight of a bright yellow BLIMP to cheer you.
    I send you support for your inertia, rage, tears
or lost feelings.
    I send you the willingness to sit with any
pain and watch it melt and change shape as
you soften. I send you a midnight
card game with someone you love, and LAUGHTER
that fills the room.
    I send you the MAJESTY of your tears
and truly
        Gentle eyes

HUGGING NATURE
letting yourself truly play outside

I WAS THE KIND of KID THAT COULD BE left in THE corner of our BACKYArd with A MAGnifying GlAss, studying ant HOMes ano Beetle pArapes.

I WAS AlSo THe kinD of KiD WHO rode Her Bike Until tired, To Discover WHAT WAS AT THE end of THE roAD.

ant HOMes + Beetle pArApes

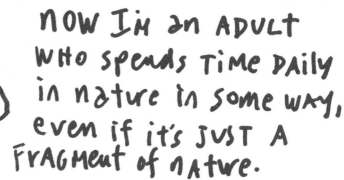

NOW I'M an ADULT WHO spenDs TIME DAILy in nature in some WAy, even if it's JUST A FrAGMeut of nAtwre.

My Brother andrew CAlls THis MY "Bouillon cuBe" lifestyle: He SAys THAT I can TAKe THe tiniest THing, and exPand it into A MUCH lArGer one.

One tiny CuBe MAKes A whole soup!

I've found that nature loves being observed and studied. I often bring home leaves or eucalyptus pods for my cat Jupiter to smell, since he stays pretty close to home. I figure that way, nature can come to him.

Letting ourselves truly play outside involves being willing to get wet, dirty or inconvenienced in some way.

So often, I hide or hibernate inside to avoid discomfort. The smells and sounds of nature are oblivious to our discomfort!

I was on a retreat in the Bahamas, and arrived to find "inclement" weather.

There are many magical and rickety stairways in San Francisco

It was chilly, rainy and very windy. I watched the sky anxiously for any change, and paced around my little place, looking out the sliding glass doors. Then I realized that if I was just (willing) (to get wet), I could probably experience miracles. So I put on a bathing suit, shorts and t-shirt and headed out to the beach.

I gasped at the lavender light peering out as the sun rose behind black storm clouds.

I quickly became accustomed to the rain and wind, and as I walked, soaking wet, it occurred to me how much this felt like swimming outside the water!

it was like the waves had gotten out of the water!

THE BEACH WAS All mine, and I WAlKeD
Until THe rain STopped. WHen I SAT Down
To eAT A few rAiSins I Found in My pockeT,
I FeLT so FUll of pleASure, and so Alive !

nature
stands
by

I want to tell you
WHAT HAppened to Me
in CentrAl pArK, in
Summer. I HAD Several
Hours in Between
interviews on My Book tour, and I HeADed
To CentrAL pArK for some "Summer relaxAtion."

AS I WAlKed into the pArK, I FeLT
My BoDy loosen, and I BreATHed More
Deeply.

THere were little white seed pUffs
Blowing THrouGH THe Air, THe sound of A
BASeBAll GAMe in THe DistAnce and
pATCHes of SunLiGHT on BriGHT Green
GrASS.

I FounD A Big rock and lAiD BACK
AGAinst it, reveLing in My surroundings.

JUST THe SiGHT of the
rock MADe Me siGH

I noticed A squirrel playing on A rock nearby, and kept watching it jump and chatter, and race up and down the rock. All of a sudden, the squirrel sat up and seemed to be staring at me, so I stared back.

Then the squirrel stood up on its hind legs, exposing its white tummy, and was really staring at me.

As I continued to look, the squirrel lifted up one little arm and

WAVED AT ME!

The waving squirrel

(O.K., he wasn't A purple squirrel)

When I shared this story with people, many were skeptical, including my brother Andrew. Later that summer, he called to tell me,

"I can't believe I'm saying this, but A squirrel waved at me yesterday, here in Berkeley!"

It was The summer of the waving squirrels. Maybe they wave all the time and we just don't see them!

I frequently forget about the unexpected pleasures in nature, and neglect to venture out even more often to experience them. It's as if I'm hypnotized by the inside delights, and can't comprehend the outside ones.

Then I find myself on a hiking trail in bright moonlight, with meteor showers overhead, and the sound of bullfrogs mating, and I'm reminded of The primitive need I have To be outside, in nature.

we

can

hug

nature

Some part of my soul relaxes when I see the "universe of nature," and I'm reminded

THAT it Doesn't need to Be MUCH, or for very long, or even very FAr Before nature touches Me.

ASK yourself These Questions:
- How Does nature touch Me?
- WHAT DO you love About nature?
- When Are you Drawn to spend time in nature?
- DO you notice A Difference when you HAven't Been in nAture?

THinGS TO Try:
- lie Down in tAll GrAss. sink in and Forget Where you Are. THen Forget your name.
- GATHer GiFTs From THe nATural world and let the stones you collect in your pockets start to pull your pants Down.
- Write A love letter To your Best Friend on A Big leAF.
- FinD A Glorious spot. sit THere and BreATHe.

JUST BreATHe

Chapter Six · Books + Quotes + Web Sights
Hugging Nature

"Plunge Boldly into the Thick of Life"
Goethe

A Walk in The Woods   By Bill Bryson

Living on The Earth   By Alicia Bay Laurel

Pilgrim At Tinker Creek   By Annie Dillard

Winter Hours   By Mary Oliver

Mango Elephants in The Sun
                    By Susana Herrera
The
Legacy of Luna   By Julia Butterfly Hill

Web Sight:
www.AliciaBaylaurel.com

"The Greatest Achievements were At First,
and for A time, Dreams. The OAK Sleeps
in The Acorn"
                J Ames Allen

I NAPPED BENEATH A Blanket
of Moss, with A FAIRY on DREAM PATROL,
and A Flower lamp shining
S O F T L Y

Dance with Color ecstatically

Vicarious pleasures
enjoying without actually moving

It is quite possible to experience a lot of pleasure without going anywhere or doing anything, except witnessing and hearing stories from others.

Vicarious pleasure is abundant, as others are always out there, experiencing new things (and sometimes I am!)

I've found a lot of satisfaction in being a "vicarious pleasure person." Here are some examples:

There is a gathering every year in the Nevada desert called Burning Man. It is dedicated to the anarchist arts, and is so astounding that I can barely describe it. Their website is: www.Burningman.com every story I hear about Burning Man is some kind of fantastic voyage.

remarkable voyages

The whole place is made up of wildly different and highly creative "villages" which are built and torn down in a very short time span. My friend Andrea brings stories of the "Glitter camp" where people lie down in child-size wading pools filled with glycerine and then have industrial-sized cans of glitter sprinkled all over their bodies.

The Glitter People

This year, I heard that they're going to build the entire camp on stilts about 15 feet off the ground, in the shape of a man, lit with neon lights and NASA will take a photo of it from outer space!

Every story I hear makes my ears tingle and my cells vibrate, yet I don't want to actually go there. I know there will be heat, and dust, and lots of dust, and inconvenience.

So... I'm a Vicarious Admirer!

It's Like my Trip to Venice, Italy.
I've Been so many Times in my imagination:

I'm wearing an iridescent purple
Cloak That skims The cobblestones as
I walk along The canals, Back to my
Candlelit villa...

Or Touch The Handblown Glass
From Murano, sip Drinks at cafes
That are Damp From The incoming Tides...

MY CAPE is WARM and Mysterious

and THen Friends Bring Me STories
of Venice:
Of creAKinG BoATS on THe canals
and narrow, lAMPLit HAllWAys, FestivAls
and cosTUMes, ecceutric Dinner pArties.

PerHAPs one DAY I will AcTUAlly Go To
Venice. It Doesut reAlly MATter, BecAge I
HAve Been THere vicAriovsly, and HAve So
enJoyeD My trips.

People love to have an eager audience for their stories and adventures. Someone who will listen avidly, and actually ask to see slides.

Vicarious pleasures can also occur on smaller, more ordinary stages. I often hear about friends going out to dinner, and feel like I was there too. I ask for details about what they ate, and imagine what I might have ordered. Sometimes, I experience several meals that way!

Experiencing pleasure through a friend's eyes also has a double advantage. You get to see his/her pleasure and feel yours too!

OH, and a lovely glass of Kunde estate's Merlot

I had crispy grilled salmon on a bed of colcannon mashed potatoes, baby beets and acorn squash

Thanks to all the people at Houstons!

Sometimes when I go out for an Adventure, I will psychically bring a friend along in my pocket, and tell him/her so. Then he/she gets the energy of my Adventure while staying home.

I am endlessly gratefull to "Armchair travel writers" except I would call it chaise lounge travel writing because I like to lie down!

These writers go, see and do things in places I would n e v e r go.

A friend in the pocket

S e r i o u s   L o u n g i n g

I just read about a rain forest expedition so fraught with danger, that I got up to shake out my blanket in case stinging scorpions had burrowed in there!

Vicarious pleasure seeking requires an actively engaged imagination. You must be able to virtually see and feel and make up your own details. You can practice this:

Begin by noticing details around you and pretend you'll be asked to describe them. I had early training in this. My grandfather ("Boppa") would send our family on trips in the summer, and ask me to keep a journal about what I saw, and then act it out for him when I got back.

I remember preparing my "Adventure Journals". I had been given such a great assignment!

MAKE YOUR OWN ADVENTURE BOOK

ADVENTURE BOOK

ODD Bits of MENUS and Tokens From MEALS on THE ROAD

There Are too many spiders in This motel and The Blankets Are really Heavy

WE SAW A BIG WATERFALL TODAY

Place where drops got onto page

WATER FAll ticket

ADMIT ONE

120

We can all be vicarious pleasure seekers and givers. When you share travels, events or adventures with friends, remember THAT THEY can then share in your JOY with you.

You can share your experiences with this in mind, in a new illuminated way.

Fairies live near my house I've seen them?

THE PAGES COULD COME ALIVE...

THINGS TO TRY:

- STRETCH your IMAGINATION BY ASKING A friend To play This GAME with you: WHAT OTHER lives could you imagine LiViNG in History or Future? MAKE up A STORY together AS THOUGH you Are THESE CHARACTERS.

- on your next ADVENTURE, collecT DETAILS specifically To SHARE with someone.

- WHERE WOULD you Like to ViCAriously TrAVEL? Describe How it smells, looks and sounds.

IMAGINATION loves To STRETCH

BOOKS, BOOKSTORES, LIBRARIES:

THE TREASURELANDS

I see BOOKS AS BiG BOUND letters TO the world. Books Guide us, nourish us and remind us of How indelibly Connected we Are.

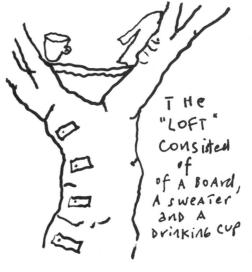

W e
A r e
A l l
so indelibly connected

I reAD every DAY, and THrive iMAGinatively inside THe pAGes. I BecAMe A writer BecAuse of reADing, and AM Always reminded of The little reADing "loFT" I BUiLT AS A CHiLD in THe BrancHes if the CraBApple Tree in My BackyArd, in THe MiDwesT.

THe "loFT" Consisted of of A BOArd, A sweAter and A DrinKing cup

123

THe library WAS My CHURCH, and I prowled THe Aisles, READING ALPHABETICALLY WHATever I Found THere. I learned to reAD very FAST, and So I searched for THe THickest BOOKs I COULD FIND.

I often slept with BOOKS, and DreAMed ABOUT WHAT I HAD reAD THAT night.

THE STACKS

i AM convinced THAT BOOKS FLY Around AT night

My friend Adrienne and I play A GAME in BOOKStores: We "SPEAK" entirely By USING BOOK titles We FIND on THe shelves. reMArKABle combinations often occur, and We Always LAUGH Boisterously.

YOU JUST PICK A title raNDomly aND THen incluDe it in A sentence

"So I MArried Adventure. AM I OLD YeT?"

I AM prone To Give BOOKS AWAY,
and USUALLY Don't inscribe THem For
THAT reason. I Like To Think of BOOKS
MOVING Freely Around The WORLD.

and Don't you JUST love
HOW BOOKS will
JUMP off of sHelves?

Of course, I Also enjoy HAVING A SMALL
library of very special BOOKS To SHAre
with people serendipitously.

I Adore libraries, and Hover in
THem, sometimes opening Books for
A particular library scent, which
I Think is A Blend of love and paper.

I Like to look AT The
little check out sHeet and
iMAGine wHo reAD THe Book
Before Me.

now THey're using computers and pHASinG
out cHeck out sHeets. I Miss THem AlreADy.

Bookstores Are anoTHer
wonderland, Full of curious
people and sHelves of Books To
Browse THrough.

OH THe MirAcles of Browsing!

I THink THAT AuTHor events Are one of
THe BeST kinds of Free, revolutionary
Activities. I'm often encHanted By
Bookstores, and wander for Hours with
Absolutely no "purpose" excepT To Book-
and-people-WATcH.

We Are so Blessed with All
of our Books

We MusT Be sure To
sHAre THese ricHes with
THe resT of THe worLD

Chapter Seven. Books + Quotes + Web Sights
Vicarious Pleasures

"The pursuit of truth and beauty is a sphere of activity in which we are permitted to remain children all our lives"

Albert Einstein

I will not die an unlived life By Dawna Markova

True Balance   By Sonia Choquette, Ph.D.

Thunder and Lightning   By Natalie Goldberg

Writing as a way of Healing
                    By Louise DeSalvo, Ph.D.

Seventeen ways to eat a mango
                    By Joshua Kadison

Spilling open   By Sabrina Ward Harrison

Web Sights:
www.newsun.com
www.sabrinawardharrison.com

"The soul should always stand ajar,
ready to welcome the ecstatic experience"
                    Emily Dickinson

SPEND LiKe A MillionAire, or not!

WiTH HARDly any Money

First, reDefine MillionAire.
More Money Does not equal More FreeDom!
We so often THINK:
"if only I HAD More Money, I could
Do _____ , or BE
_____ . "

Your Money reAlly isnt your life.
We Become seDuced By the illusion of
(MORE) and ForGeT ABout (WHO) we really Are.

YOU Are SAFe no MATTer How Much
Money you HAve, or Dont HAve.
Our essential sAFety lies in Much
Deeper places THan Money.

MUCH Deeper

I believe THAT THere is More room for people To experiment with living "As if" they have Money, and also "As if" they don't.

if you Are craving experiences THAT you perceive THAT people with Money Are HAving, partake vicariously or peripherally of some of those Things.

"Attend" events As A Bystander, onlooker, urban Adventurer. Kindly and consciously invite yourself into environments THAT you wouldn't ordinarily partake of.

Have no expectations!

WHATever The Money we're All simply people

The "HAves" and The "HAve-nots" Are ancient clubs THAT need Membership re·vision. if you compare yourself to others and FinD THAT you HAve less...

less WHAT? Besides Money

I spent years studying unhappy millionaires, and found that their money made them unhappier.

not the money itself, the <u>experience</u> of money... or, the one they chose!

You might be thinking, "Fine! Give some to me!"

But I assure you that if you don't do the necessary psychological foundational work, you would be unhappy too!

I've lived as a "starving artist" and outside the money system, bartering and trading. I've lived on other people's money, by the largesse of my parents and society. (welfare, food stamps) and through hundreds of low-paying jobs.

I now invest my money and time in my own company, which assists in serving society.

let Money

move you

to serve

I've Been Able to travel and visit places THAT were previously unknown To Me, A Bit More eAsily and often. I BrinG you This Message From the "land of luxury" if you HAvent Been there yet.

It can Be cloying, Boring and BADly Designed!

I've Discovered THAT some of The "BEST" plAces Are Devoid of spirit and Joy. If your soul is AGitAted, it is MUCH worse in luxury-land. I Know, BecAuse This WAS AlwAys My refuGe,

" if only I CoulD eAT _____ , or Go _____ or Attend _____ or weAr _____ . "

Once I experienced some of these things, I quickly Discovered How Flimsy and FAlse THey CoulD Be.

D E E P P E A C E

is an inside JoB

So WHAT DO you DO if you're reADING this and still feel left out, poverty stricken, CRABBy or UNDeserving?

First, you Are not Alone. Second, consider studying Money As an energy system and yourself in relation to it. If there Are experiences you want, Find Alternative wAys to Be There. Offer your services, Appeal to phiLanthropy, Design A program THAT includes YOU.

Here's How I can contribute to your _____.
I can specifically offer These Things: _____.
It will Benefit you in THese wAys: _____.

It isn't enough to just HAve the "HAves" Give TO THe "HAve-nots." BOTH Groups MUst Be educated To Know wHy/How.

THere is so much more room for
WEALTH-SHARING. We need BRIGHT, committed
SOULS TO WORK on THiS!

We need
BRiGHT GLOWinG
SOULS FOR
THiS WORK

We need to REACH ARMS and legs Across
the GAPS and include everyone WHo
WISHes to Be included. We MUST Also
FiGure out A WAY to HeLP THose
WHo DON'T KNOW HOW to Be included.

let conscious service Be TAUGHT in SCHOOLS

"TO WANT TO HeLP everyone in
everyTHinG is To SUCCUMB to violence.
THe Frenzy of the ACTiVisT neutraLizes
His or Her WORK for peACe"
                    THOMAS Merton

It is Time To:

- reDefine Millionaire As A Measurement of The spirit
- expand our consciousness to include new perspectives on Money and WHAT iT is in our lives
- remove identifications of WEALTH By refusing To Honor Status Symbols
- SHAre Money and knowledge Creatively and BOLDly
- re·Design The Money!

Spend Like A Millionaire, or not!

"The proper utilization of our intelligence and knowledge is to effect changes from within, to develop a good heart"

the DALAI LAMA

Faith Works By Jim Wallis

True prosperity By SHAKTI GAWAIN

Sex and Money Are Dirty, Aren't They?
By Cheri Huber

Creating Money By Sanaya Roman and Duane Packer

Sometimes enough is enough By MARSHA Sinetar

Spirit Matters By Michael Lerner

WEB SIGHTS:
www.keepitsimplebooks.com
www.sojo.net

"No pessimist ever discovered the secret of the stars, or sailed to uncharted land or opened a new doorway for the human spirit"
Helen Keller

Pleasure in Being Consciously Single

Like a cheese slice!

Truly choosing to be single is very different from being single and looking for a partner, or just waiting for one.

After ending a long-term relationship, I realized that I had never chosen to be single, it had just happened.

So I embarked on a real love affair with myself, A MAD PASSIONATE ONE

MY OWN PLEASURE CRAFT

WHICH involved HAVING A very SINGULAR Focus on myself and my CAPACity for

Self·Love

I HAD ALWAYS BEEN AFRAID to explore self·love for FEAR of WHAT I WOULD FIND, or not FIND THERE.
or BEING THOUGHT of as SELFISH!

Also, WHO WOULD I BE without

SOMEONE

To love?

COULD I really STOP "looking" and JUST look AT MY self? and, if I WAS not enough For MySelf, How COULD I BE enough For another?

COULD I BE MY(own)

SOMEONE?

I DIDN'T FIND very MUCH support for THIS APPROACH in Society, So I

Found systems of HEALING and Discovery THAT WOULD support my SEARCH and inquiry. I Discovered A lot of pAin and pleasure on my journey of leArning How to love myself.

I felt the pAin of finding even more FlAws and splendid imperfections Than I'd ever THOUGHT.

some Definitely not splendid!

I SAW THE "GIFTS" of All of my poor CHoices and Misguided relationships, and FeLt the FeAr I uncovered WHen I really looked in The mirror and sAid

no posing

I love you

WHAT I Heard and SAW in response scared and sAddened Me. It HAS taken A lot of Time and work to Be Able to look AT myself in The mirror with compAssion and

SEE ONLY LOVE

and it HAppens intermittently

THE PLEASURE HAS BEEN in FINDING MYSELF SO precious and lovABLE. I WAS AMAZED to witness How endEARING I CAN BE. I'M A TenDer little BEAN!

I AM learning still, How to Feel Deserving of this self. love. I'M Also SolidiFYing MY TRUST in LiFe, and in MY self.

love swirling Around me

i
CAN now
Truly SAy
THAT I experience
More Moments
of loving My
self

THis Brings me GreAT JOY

of course I Also HAVe HUGe ArguMents with Myself...

I AM Also AWARe THAT THis self-love will Be tested wHen/if I enter into A romantic relationship AGAin. THe Mirror THAT is HeLD up By another is A very Different KIND of reflection. or AT leAST A Different angle

YeT my FOUNDATioNAL self-love work HAS provided Me with A BASis I've never HAD Before. I intend to keep Delving Deeply into the pleasures of Being consciously single, and live vicariously THrovGH my partnered Friends. I stuDy THese relationships like A sociAL scientist, and MArveL THAT anyone GeTs Along with anyone!

The SHAreD Mirror

I'm not sure THAT any conventionAL relationship will work for Me, or whether I want to explore one...

I DiD write A PAGe LoNG personAL AD!

I'm still Discovering so MUCH ABout myself. we will see...

p.s. I'm looking For A MAle lesBian

140

Chapter nine· Books + Quotes + Web Sights
Consciously single

"Ask a difficult question and the
marvelous answer appears"
                    Rumi

<u>I</u> <u>promise</u> <u>Myself</u>   By Patricia Lynn Reilly

<u>A</u> <u>year</u> <u>By</u> <u>The</u> <u>Sea</u>   By Joan Anderson

<u>When</u> <u>you</u> <u>eat</u> <u>at</u> <u>the</u> <u>refrigerator,</u> <u>pull</u> <u>up</u> <u>A</u> <u>chair</u>
                    By Geneen Roth

<u>The</u> <u>little</u> <u>Book</u> <u>of</u> <u>letting</u> <u>Go</u>
                    By Hugh Prather

<u>imagine</u> <u>A</u> <u>woman</u> <u>in</u> <u>love</u> <u>with</u> <u>Herself</u>
                    By Patricia Lynn Reilly

Web Sights:
www.goodvibes.com
www.drnorthrup.com
www.velvetjanes.com

Music: Donovan sutras
       Velvet Janes

"I took a deep breath and listened to the
old brag of my heart. I am, I am, I am"

                    Sylvia Plath

stories and examples of pleasure

THE TARTS

There is a most succulent Group of women

who have been meeting for 8 years in Eugene, Oregon. They call themselves The Tarts. They have their own Dictionary and lexicon of words and Definitions. For instance:

FATHers of TArts: poptArts
Husbands of TArts: pArts
TArt in trouble: TiT
Car Appetizers: CAr-Derves

They speak of Being OLD Together, and Being Able to wipe AwAy eACH other's Drool. Their Bond is sturdy and Beautiful to see. I met Them and ADored THem instantly, and LAughed So HArd My stomACH ACHed.

Thank you Vivienne, DiAnA, Jean and MAY-Ree! I loved visiting your TArtDom!

I'd love To visit AGAin

Little notes

As I traveled Around the country
On my 23-city book tour, I became Aware
of the need to share A particular message
with people, and Decided to Do this with
little notes THAT I wrote in ADVance.

The note said:

Tiny note From

SARK
reAD it
refolD it
pAss it on

Tiny notes For people's souls

and THen you opened it up, and it said:

You are seen

You are known

You are loved

I wrote this because so many people
feel invisible, unknown and unlovable.
I also did it because I loved writing notes
in school.

These little notes on my tour caused a
lot of pleasure for me, and for other people.

So many miracles happened:

In vermont, the audience of 300 began
writing similar notes and passing them
around! They wrote: You are so beautiful to me!

In Martha's vineyard, the ups delivery
man asked if he could read it, and with
tears of joy, asked if he could keep it.

At one event, a young man took the
note and left the bookstore!

I would usually ask
if there was someone
in the audience who
felt in need of the note.

A special need for extra love...

The exact
person would
materialize
who most needed it

Some one would usually claim it
with certainty.
    I think THere's A lot of power and
pleAsure in tiny, unexpected communications.
I've Begun carrying little notes with
me wherever I go, and Handing
THem out

We can
All traveL
with tiny
notes
and
Hand
THem
out
in
All
Sorts of situations

More stories + examples of pleasure

I knew that my Dad had had a best friend, and his name was Ed. I also knew that Ed lived in portland oregon, and I planned to see him on my book tour. Since my Dad's death, I really wanted to hear Ed's stories about him.

Then my mom called to tell me that Ed had died.

I felt such regret at not just calling him earlier. Now it felt like such a loss. My Mother said, "remember that you have first cousins in portland and Eugene..."

I interrupted her.

"Give me their numbers and I'll call them now!"

I hadn't seen these cousins in 40 years, and had no idea what to expect.

I called them up

My cousin Jim and his wife, Sally, were instantly enthusiastic about seeing me, and revealed that ED HAD BEEN sending them my books and writing letters about me for years!

JIM + SALLY HAVE NEAT KIDS too!

ED WASN'T AS DEAD AS I ORIGINALLY THOUGHT!

Suddenly I found myself sitting at a Red Lobster restaurant in Portland with a whole tribe of Kennedys!

We had similar habits too: ordering water with no ice, refusing to wear logos on clothing, heel problems, and outspokenness...

I was amazed to discover that I had "brand-new" relatives and felt such JOY at the discovery.

Then I met my cousins in Eugene, Bill and May-Ree. I HAD already met their beautiful daughters in Eugene...

We started dinner at 10 p.m., and were still eating, talking and laughing at 2 a.m.!

candles
good red wine
salmon grilled
vegetables and sharing of soul stories

148

MY DAD WAS Bill's FAV
and He WAS BURSTING wi'
Detailed, color. Full storie
Jim and Bill HAD DeArly l
     it WAS A wHole new look

    Bill SAID,
  "OH, He TAUGHT Me How to w.
POOL and CHeAT AT it, and How 7
GOOD service in A restaurant!"
I FELT SVCH AWe AT HeARING "new stories" ABout My
every word WAS precious ...

    Bill sHAred this story ABoUT His LiFe:
He is now A retired Homicide Detective

    Bill's pArtner WAS MurDered. He stopped
workiNG and started HAviNG nightMAres.
with some unexpected Free time on His Hands,
He went to The LocAL Hospital and Asked
ABout CUDDLiNG preMAture BABies.

Tiny BABies neeD LArGe Love

soman
"we've n
Before ...
Bill re
need
well
Be
He

AT THE HospitaL saiD,

...ver HAD A MaLe BaBy cuddler

...plied thAt the new BABies WouLD

...ove and Affection From A man As

...As A Woman, and Asked if He couLD

...the FirsT. and So, For Months BiLL

...LD All the BABies THAT needed love,

...and they HeALed HiM. He WAS ABLe to

recover and return to work.

I Feel such KinDred spirit-ship with

my "new" Kennedy relations, and AM So

GrateFul To HAve FouNd them.

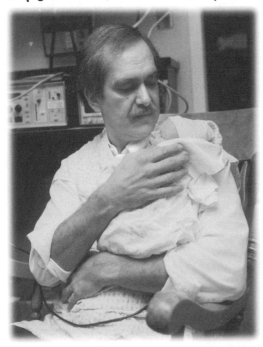

THiS is BiLL

CUDDLiNG

A

B A B Y

or

A B A B Y

CUDDLiNG

B i l l !

♡

Grace

I AM sitting AT Dinner AT A restaurant
CAlled Chez panisse, in Berkeley, CALifornia.
I notice A tiny girl come in with 3 women.
She is ABout 4 yeArs OLD, BAre foot, Little
BlAck Bangs, and weArinG A Flowered
Sleeveless summer Dress.

There wAs A lovely
energy AT Their tAble, and
Around Her. it FeLt Like
A GLow.

I HeArd Them cAll Her GrAce,
So I pulled out my purple pen
and Drew Her an angel on THe
WHite Butcher pAper on my tAble.

The angel wAs
HoLDING A sign
THAT SAID,

"GrAce is So
Deeply loved"

THen I DATeD the DRAWiNG aud Delivered
it to Their tABle. it was odd, Because I Dont usually DAte DrawiNGS

one of The women tooK it aud ThanKed
Me, with tears in Her eyes, Which surprised
Me until sHe said,

"ThanK yu so MuCH. THis Means More than
you KNow. GRACE's ADoption JusT Became
Final

TODAY,
aud We DiDnt even Know if it WOULD.
We're Going To FRAMe THis little angel ..."

PAY
Attention
to
angels

One soft summer evening, I went with my brother into the Berkeley Hills to watch him at swimming practice.

After watching for a while, I wandered up into the twilit woods, and found an enormous tree, partially fallen, and growing into the hillside.

I clambered out onto one of the widest, friendliest branches and lay there, breathing in the dark and leaves. I played horizontal hide-and-seek with the newly risen moon...

THE MOTHER TREE

I visited my Brother's Apartment spontaneously one day. At that time, He was living in a slightly less ordered environment than I'm comfortable with, and His style has caused some small sibling tensions between us.

On this day, I felt determined not to mention any "mess" that I saw, especially since I was a drop-in visitor. As I picked my way through His Bedroom to the Bed where I intended to take a tiny nap, I stopped to stare at the wild tangle of objects on and in the Bed.

There was a path through the wild tangle

He chuckled as He watched me, and I said cheerfully,
"Don't worry! I can just lie on this side!"
As I pulled a piece of Blanket over me,

I HEARD something crunching under my shoulder. I reached behind and pulled out an enormous, FAMILY SIZED bag of tortilla chips!

We both froze.

I reached in and pulled out A chip.

"OH GOOD! Your bed HAS everything in it THAT anybody could want!"

I watched His FACE soften. I felt such pure pleasure THAT I didnt start criticizing As I usually would.

It felt like an old FAMILY pattern HAD Been Broken in THAT moment.

OLD
PATTern
JUDGMENT
SMASHED

pleasures of Zoe

My godchild Zoe is 6 years old although I'm positive her soul is much older.

One night we sat on the hill by my house and she asked me how I was feeling. I told her that I was sad, and she said,

"Oh Susan. Are you forgetting to stay in JUST TODAY, and trying to GO AHEAD TO TOMORROW?"

Another day, she danced wildly to the music of 10,000 maniacs and breathlessly said, she also asked if there were really 10,000 maniacs!

"I could really twirl forever you know!"

We sat together in my cottage, spilling our snacks, and laughing at my cat Jupiter sneaking past. Zoe suddenly said,

"Can you describe what romance is?"

Jupiter sneaks past

I talked about WOOING, and YEARNING, and her parents' love for each other, and she sighed and leaned back.

"I think THAT love is my favorite thing in this whole world..."

Me too, Zoe,
Me too.

I WALKED UP TO TWO little GiRLS ON THE
BEACH, Bent over AT THE WAIST, looking AT
the ocean WAVES. I Joined Them, and
imitated their posture. We All started
LAUGHING. no words, JUST LAUGHING.

People Are so prepAred to welcome
Moments of pleAsure.

I compLiMented the Food service worker
AT the Airport on the cute Bottle of MILK
I WAS Buying, and sHe Grinned and
replied,

"OH I Know! I Just _love_ these
little MiLK Bottles!"

A DorAble
MiLK
Bottles

I stopped A Man with GorGeous
COBALT-BIve luGGAGE To compLiment THE
color, and He Didn't speAk enGLISH. We
Finally Figured out How to communiCATE
with Gestures and He BeGan exclAiming

"Sí! Colores! Sí!"

I HAVE THIS
MARVeloUS pAiR of
AQUA BAGS THAT I've
HAD For (So) MAny yeArs.
Now They're DisinteGrating...
THe Pockets Are HeLo SHUT with BreAd ties

I love over hearing tidbits of conversation. Two older women, carrying straw luggage and wearing smart-looking hats said to each other,

"Those flights from Bombay are just hideous! They all leave at 3 a.m... which is a preposterous hour!"

There can be such pleasure in witnessing humanity, if we can release our attachments to order and safety, and what is "usually done." If we can boldly and sensitively speak up, miracles can, and will, occur.

I was having breakfast at my favorite spot in San Francisco.

We all deserve a spot

It's my favorite because they take reservations for one, recognize my voice when I call, and save my favorite table by the front window.

THey Also MAKe perfect eGGS, except
of course, on certAin splendidly imperfect DAys.
  on This DAy, I SAT Drinking My Fresh-squeezed
GrApeFruit Juice and overheard A womAn AT The
next TABle sAy,
  "SAn FrAncisco is of course, the Most MARvelous!"
  I couldn't resist, and leaned over to sAy,
  "SAn FrAncisco is THe Best!"
  THese 3 women were A writer's Group and
invited Me To Join THem.
  We TALKed ABout JeAlousy, and AGinG,
and writing and All the DepTHs THAT uncommon
women can explore.
  So Much LAUGHTer wAS SHAred

M o lly , MAGGie, illene, susan

I ASKed if I could BE A visitor To Their writer's Group, and they said Y e S.

So FAr, I've spent severAl profound Hours With These women, Who Are All writing and creating, and living THeir lives in

P leAsurABle SiGnificance

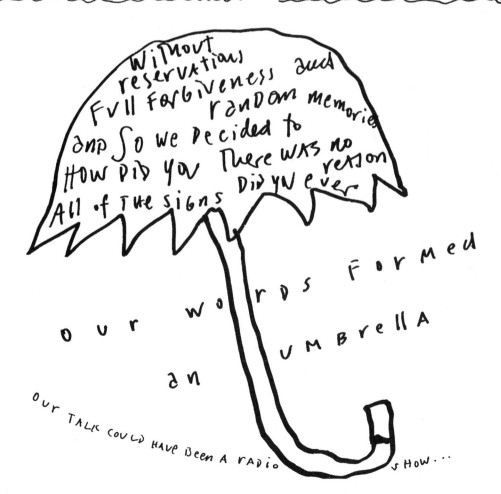

without
reservations
Full Forgiveness and
random memories
and So we Decided to
How Did you There wAs no
All of The signs Did you ever reason

o u r w o r D s F o r M e d

a n u M B r e l l A

Our TALK could HAve Been A rAdio Show...

"Liquid poetry" is WHAT I SAID to describe MY FIRST WATSU MASSAGE THERAPY Session. I'D BEEN ATTRACTED to the METHOD for YEARS, After it WAS Developed AT HARBIN Hot SPriNGS in CALIFORNIA.

The BASic concept is THIS: MASSAGE in WATER. You Are FLOATED, CrADled, stretched and supported BY A PRACTITIONER WHO GUIDES you into VArious positions in A WARM (98°) POOL of WATER.

I'm STARTING to Be ABle to try More THINGS Without THINKING SO MUCH ABOUT THEM, SO ON A REMARKABLY SUNNY DAY in SAN Francisco, I CAlled the NUMBER for The AQUATIC MASSAGE Center and spoke To A MAN named "rAiNBOW HEART."

Since one of MY Middle NAMES is rAiNBOW, I KNEW it WAS A GOOD BEGINNING.

Before MY AppoiNTMENT, A Few THOUGHTS FlOATED into View:

WHAT if ...

WOULD I BE WARM ENOUGH?
WOULD I HAVE SENSUAL/SEXUAL THOUGHTS?
WOULD HE?
WOULD I GET WATER IN MY NOSE?
WOULD IT REALLY AFFECT ME, RELAX ME,
EASE MY SORE MUSCLES?
WOULD MY BATHING SUIT RIDE UP MY BUTT,
OR FALL OFF MY SHOULDERS?

WHEN I ARRIVED FOR MY APPOINTMENT, RAINBOW
HEART GREETED ME AND WE DID AN INTAKE SESSION.
ONE OF THE QUESTIONS WAS ABOUT DIET AND EXERCISE,
AND I RESPONDED,

"I EAT CONSCIOUSLY AND MOVE JOYFULLY"

(OF COURSE UNLESS I GO UNCONSCIOUS AND DON'T MOVE AT
ALL WHILE OVEREATING...)

WHEN HE ASKED WHAT I DID FOR A LIVING, I
SHOWED HIM A COPY OF MY BOOK Transformation Soup.
HE LAUGHED AND SAID HE HAD JUST BOUGHT
MY BOOK CHANGE your life without Getting out of BeD.

I SAID THAT WE WERE KINDRED SPIRITS AND
WE SPOKE ABOUT BEING IN THE WOMB. I SAID,

"I loved it IN THE WOMB!"

and we BOTH SAID SiMULTANEOUSLY,
"I DIDN'T want to come out!"

So now, BEING WOMBMATES, we proceeded
To His specially BUILT POOL, REDWOOD DECK
and tiny JAPANESE GARDEN.

He Supported ME
From BeHIND,
and BEGAN THE
Session with A
Connecting TOUCH
To THE BACK of MY
HEAD, and explAiNED
THAT I would lean
BACK, and He WOULD
"FLOAT ME OUT."

WE
BECAME
JUST
SHAPES
iN
THE
POOL

From THAT Moment
ON, I DID NOTHING else
THAT resemBLED effort.

it WAS complete surrender

I Closed my eyes and felt my Body
Moving in slow circles Like A Dancer, in
exquisite slow Motion, LiMBS AKiMBO,
i've Always loved THAT word AKiMBO
and opening various "Doors" and "windows"
in my BODY. It MADe Me THINK of A phrase
From A FAvorite song
    "Just lean BACK and let love CArry
    Jov Along"

J o y
of
Cooking
GreAT Music

    I BeGan To Cry, THinking of
the enormous Bond we HAve with
our Mothers from THAT watery ride in
the womB.
    I Felt no urge to speak, which is rare,
since I often rely HeAvily on the verBAL
Aspects.
    I BeGan to lose TrAcK of the edges
of the pool, and wonder if perHaps
I HAD FLoAted into A Much larGer BODY
of water.
                Much larGer

165

I could tell That stretching of my Body was Taking place, yet it wasn't from "my" efforts. I wondered OCCASIONALLY if I was doing anything AT All, or should Be. (my attachment to results)

At The end of our session, He suddenly released me To Float off on my own, and I couldn't tell if I was still Being Held!

I would Be BACK for More.

P.S. answers To The questions I posed at The Beginning

· I was warm enough, ALThough once my Big Toe Got chilly
· I had sensual Thoughts, Felt no sexual ones from Me or him, it Felt very professional
· no water Got into my nose
· it Deeply relaxed me, and eased my sore muscles
· my Bathing suit stayed in place, and once or twice He surreptitiously pulled up A strap

When I Got Home, I Fell Helplessly Asleep for A 4-Hour nap.

A Deep nap

There is a place in Portland, Oregon, called Rimsky-Korsakoffee. It is a most unusual cafe, and I went there late one evening with my friend Vanessa and her boyfriend, Mark. The cafe is in an old house on a residential street. I didn't see any signs for it, except this one on the door:

> Usually open til midnight although our hours are flexible... Are you?

We sat around a low, round table and studied the scribbly menus. It immediately felt like a place to tell and hear stories, and I fell into kind of a trance.

Then I noticed that we weren't getting service, and Vanessa said brightly,

"That's what the ping-pong balls are for!"

if you need us just use these ping-pong balls

in the Middle of the table is a little bucket filled with ping-pong balls, which you fling at the walls or door of the kitchen to get attention!

I promptly flung balls at the kitchen door, and a cheerful person instantly appeared.

Many of the things on the Menu weren't available,

What if ping-pong balls were available everywhere for flinging!

yet in My trance state, it simply didn't Matter.

When tea and dessert arrived, I noticed that the design on the table top seemed to have changed. When I looked again, my teapot seemed to have moved!

Mysterious things were happening!

Now, I WAS STARING AT THE TABLE, and Vanessa and MARK were CHUCKLING.

THE TABLE WAS MICROSCOPICALLY revolving!

All The DISHES were inching Around The tABLE!

Then I remembered Some of The stories I'D Heard About The place... Some tABLes Go lower, or Higher, Some simply stArt DisAppearing into The WALL!

I, ADored The eccentricity of it All, and it reminded Me of How little we reALLY play with our surroundings, and How MUCH More we could.

I won't reveal More of The UNUSUAL Things AT RiMsky's... You can Go THere, or reAD ABOut it!

The RiMsky CHronicles + opERATiNG ManuAL an anthology edited By Gilliun nance

truly eccentric Conversation and levitating Teacups!

GOODY CABLE

To order Book or visit CAFE: 503. 232. 2640 707 s.e. 12th portland oregon 97214

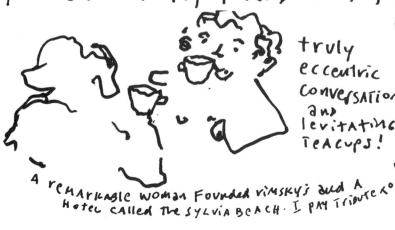

A reMArkABle woman Founded riMsky's and A Hotel cAlled The SYLViA BEACH. I PAY Tribute To

I WAS in the Tropics with My DeAr Friend Adrienne, and sHe WAS leAving Before My BirthDAY. SO, I WOULD BE Alone on My BirthDAY in THis roMantic resort. I wrote in My JournAL:

My FeAr is THAT I will end up Being All Alone AT A Tipping TABle, with A candle that keeps going out and A sullen waiter...

THe night of My BirthDAY, I Arrived At the cAndleLit, outDoor Buffet Dinner and iMMediAtely noticed that everyone WAS with SoMeone.

everyone But Me!
The MAître d´ Motioned to A tABle, and it WAS A tiny TABle AgAinst the WALL, neAr the BATHrooM, with A FlickeriNG candle!

Just Like WHAT I'd written in My JournAL!

TABle of DooM

I SAID, "no thank you, I'm meeting someone"

and WALKED off, My HEArt pounding, looking for A friendly FACE.

I SAW A group of ADULts WEARing Winnie-the-pooH BirTHDAY HATS! I WALKed up and ASKed whose BirthDAY it WAS.

"It's mine!" A Man cHeerily announced and I SAID,

"It's Mine too!"

cHeery little HATS

THey produced another HAT and invited Me to sit Down. We exchanged stories of WHAt We DID For A living. When I revealed THAT I WAS SARK, They All leapt up From the tAble, Knocking over their CHAirs.

"We're All teACHErs! We Use your BOOKS in our classrooms!"

We TALKed until THE candles Burned low and THE Moon rose HigH

CHAPTER TEN: BOOKS + QUOTES + WEB SIGHTS
STORIES and EXAMPLES of pleasure

"the MOST revolutionary Act one can commit in our world is to Be HAPPY"
Hunter "PATCH" ADAMS

The seeker's guide   BY ELIZABETH Lesser

Living in THE LIGHT of DEATH:
on THE Art of Being Truly Alive   By larry rosenberg

escaping into The open   BY ELIZABETH Berg

HOW TO DRAW A CLAM   By Joy siKorsKi

The rule of TWO   By ann Woodin
DRAWings By andrew RUSH

sweet Zen   By CHeri HuBer

WEB SIGHT:
WWW. CAMPSARK. Com

"I HAVE spread My DreAMs under your feet; treAD softly BecAuse you treAD on My DreAMs"
W. B. YEATS

I SEND TO YOU...

Twin star lilies in a crystal vase

The sight of a baby hippo, just born

Pygmy music from north Africa

Brand new underwear

One deluxe violin serenade

Tiny seashells in a toddler's hand

Jewel-tone glass bottles

A private poetry recital, just for you

Homemade biscuits with soft butter

The applause of your ancestors

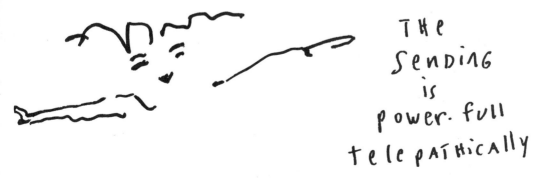

The
sending
is
power-full
telepathically

Sending out pleasures to the world

As we expand our ability to experience and remember pleasure, it is good to share the pleasure by "sending it" to other people. Begin now to invent pleasures to send.

I send to you...

rememBer wHen...

You would do THAT Little Hop·step·skip
To get synchronized with your best Friend
or your MoM?

You cracked the double popsicle in HALf
To give to your Friend?

You didn't plan to do
THings, you Just did THings!

I Always Liked the Banana ones

Your Friend invited you
To dinner, and you didn't HAve To
Be polite, you Just said, "WHAT Are you
HAving?"

You BABY JAT, and All the FooD in their
refrigerAtor and cupBoArds seemed
MirAculous?

When stAring AT rAindrops on A windoW WAs
Compelling entertAinment?

You could sHout
To your Friend,
"you're not the
BoSS of Me!"

"you're not THe BoSS of Me!"

I remember...
These particular pleasures

WALKING BAREFOOT ON SQUASHED CRABAPPLES in the GRASS, in MY BACKYARD

MARVELING AT MY Brother's snapping Turtle THAT WAS ABLE TO SNAP A THICK stick in HALF

leaning SOLIDLY AGAINST MY MOM During CHURCH, praying for sleep or escape

lAunching my own little plastic BOAT in the creek, and FLOATING DOWNSTREAM, WATCHING the Trees Go BY

losing my turtle, OBADIAH, for months and then FINDING HIM in the BACK of the closet still Alive, even Though he'd HAD no food or WATER For so long

MAKING an entire MONOPOLY GAME From SCRATCH, with cardBoard and MARKERS

i
Adored
MY
turtle

remembering past pleasures

In order to increase our pleasure capacity today, it is important to keenly remember pleasures from our past. Begin now to describe pleasures you remember, in as much detail as possible.

I remember:

IMAGINE THIS:

YOU ARRIVE BY SMALL BOAT, AT A TROPICAL island. A SMILING MAN GREETS YOU AND LEADS YOU BENEATH A CANOPY OF PINK HIBISCUS FLOWERS, THROUGH AN OPEN-AIR LIVING ROOM LOBBY, AND INTO A SMALL ELECTRIC CART, WHICH TAKES YOU TO YOUR COTTAGE BY THE SEA.

YOUR COTTAGE HAS A LARGE BED COVERED WITH BRIGHTLY COLORED BATIK FABRIC, AND IS BENEATH A SLOWLY SPINNING CEILING FAN.

DOUBLE FRENCH DOORS ARE OPEN TO THE OCEAN, WHICH GLEAMS TURQUOISE THROUGH THE PALM FRONDS.

GLEAMS TURQUOISE THROUGH THE PALM FRONDS

You HAVE your own private BeACH PATH with a Handpainted sign. You follow this PATH to The seA, wHere you FinD A Horse and rider on the BeACH. The Horse weArs no SADDle, and it rises out of the Ocean, GListening BeneATH it's rider.

Private BeACH PATH

You see A place to lie Down

A SOFT SPOT

You sleep
and
D reA M,
FloATing
in the SOFT
Tropical Air.

You AWAKen JUST AS THE LIGHT is FADing and TORCH LiGHTS

Are Lit...

IMAGINE THIS:

A BOAT TAKES you to MARTHA'S VINEYARD, and you are taken to a small flower-covered inn where everyone knows your name.

Your bedroom in the old house is in the corner with dormer windows. There is a pale yellow duvet on the bed, and the tops of trees outside the windows.

A red bicycle is parked outside, just for you. It has big balloon tires, and a puffy wide seat, a bell and a basket.

Best Bike

The town is tiny, with little flower-filled lanes leading to the ocean. At a small bookshop in the first floor of a Victorian house, you buy a novel, and ride your red bike back to the inn. There is a tea tray outside your room with a big slice of chocolate cake.

Big piece of CAKE

Then, it's time for a nap.

OH BLESS THE HOB KNOB!

iMAGine THiS:

A GUEST HOME SO COMPLETE THAT you
Are sure you ACTUALLy Live in it?
   LAvender in sunshine, GODDESS STATUES
DrAped in tiny leAves, A DouBle-wide cHAiSe
lounge in Front of A WOOD-BurninG FirePLACE.
A cHenille BlankeT, HEALinG BOOKS and
CD's. AH, the luxury of HAnd Blown GLASS
and Crooked pottery DiSHes. Flowers tucked
into All the corners, an orchid in the KiTCHen.
   THe Bed is Aimed AT THE SUN SeT
Like THE prow of A Joft SHip···
   SwinGs and HAMMocKS, tinKLinG Bells.
   You sit in A wide Wooden CHAir
and WATCH AS A

               W H A le
leAps out of the wATer.

if I
WAS A
YOUnG
WHAle
I WOULD

Lick THe
SALt off My
TeeTH and Blow
WATer Like A
TruMPeT

You write A
poem in your
JOurnAL

181

CHApter eleven: Books + Quotes + web siGHTs

I send you...

"Tell me WHAT it is you plan to Do with Your one wiLD and precious Life"

MAry OLiver

Suffering is <u>optionAl</u> By CHeri HUBer

<u>You ALreADy Know WHAT Io DO</u>

By SHAron FraNQueMonT

<u>FeArless creAting</u> By eric MAiJel, PH.D.

<u>How Io GeT From wHere you Are</u>
<u>Io wHere you want Io Be</u>

By CHeri HUBer

<u>The Four Agreements</u> By Don MiGueL RUiz

WeB SiGHT:
WWW.BereALMAG.com

"MAn is not Free to refuse TO DO the THinG
WHicH Gives Him More pleaJure THan anything
else"

SteNDHAL

nor is A WomAn!

pleAsure   mentors

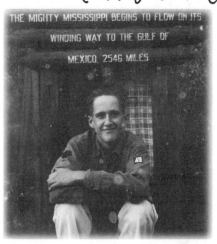

THE MIGHTY MISSISSIPPI BEGINS TO FLOW ON ITS WINDING WAY TO THE GULF OF MEXICO. 2546 MILES

ART

My DAD, Art, Brought Awareness of pleAsure To My life First By cocreating Me! and second, By His sense of HUMor, LAUGHTer and eAGerness to "Go-see-Do!"

He Also HAD some HABits THAT fortified My commitment to pleAsure. He WAS the AutoMAtic NO sAyer in the FAMily. His First iMPULse WAS To protect and proceed cArefully. He Also traveled A lot and DiDn't Know Which things To sAy no and yes to.

So we leArned to Go ASK MOM, BecAuse sHe usuAlly sAid yes!

My FAther's no-sAyinG Acted As A sort of reverse role MoDel for Me. I turned To eMBvAce every pleAsure thAt cAMe AlonG, in counterpoint To WHAT I perceived As His resistance to pleAsure.

MUCH of His resistance WAS Generational, and lAter, HEAlTh related.

As He AGed, we HAD More conversations About pleasure, and I Began to Discover More About WHAT GAve HiM JOY. I Found out tHAT He loved to Color, I AlreADY knew He loved to DRAW and started sending HiM BlaNk MandAlAs to Fill with Color.

He AMused HiMself By SigNing them "Art By Art," BecAUse He kNew I SigNed Mine "Art By SARK."

MY DAD WAS the kind of Guy tHAt PromoteD pleASure BeHiND the sceNes. He WOULD HAVE MY MOM Give Me Money, or suGGestions for FUn, and you WOULDN'T kNow it HAD come FroM HiM.

SneAkY DAD

I remember all the popsicles and car trips, houseboat and canoe trips, games of tag at the lake, and so many truly fun moments with my dad. His sense of humor was outer-directed, so most people would say how fun and funny he was. That was true, and I also witnessed the shy and sensitive guy whose pleasures came from tiny moments in the family. Like napping!

When he was dying in hospice care, I heard that they were asking him if they could get him anything, and he laboriously said,

"A Mar...ti...ni..."

They weren't able to find all the ingredients in time, but I'm sure he's enjoying a fine cigar and perfectly made martini somewhere.

andrew

WHen MY Brother andrew WAS Born, I THOUGHT I WOULD Die of pleAsure. I WAS 11 yeArs oLD, and couLDnt iMAGine

Me AT 13, anDreW AT 2. He's WeAring A DiAper on His HeAD As pArt of A pirAte CostuMe, with A rubBer Band HoLDing it on

A Better toy than an anDrew. WATCHing HiM Grow up, GrADuAte From College and Become A teAcHer HAS Been one of the Most enDuring Joys of My life.

THis is His First yeAr of teACHing (9th GrADe SociAL stuDies AT A pubLic SCHOOL in OAkland, CALiforniA) and the cLoCk in the cLAssrooM is Broken. So anDrew TApeD A piece of construction PAper over it and Wrote on it

This photo shows early Determination!

n oT
TiMe
YeT

Photo by leigh taylor at white bear lake

andrew introduced me to the pleasures of BOWLING! He practices WHAT I CALL "zen BOWLING." He calls it "BOWL your cares AWAY."

Somehow, He got me to join A BOWLING league! This is Astonishing, since I Don't plan AHead Socially, and Don't usually enjoy These types of Activities. I Agreed for the love of my Brother.

I LOVED iT !

We were called the BOWLWEEVILS and I Won A Trophy !!! (ALTHOUGH it WAS only BECAUSE I HAD the Highest score JUMP of the women in the league: 90 To 140)

Andrew brings pleasure into my life almost every day. His perspective of life and wise words are usually delivered in a certain kind of CACKLING way because he knows I love THAT type of humor.

Bless Andrew as a teacher!

P.S. I wrote about my brother in my book Succulent WILD WOMAN, and horrified him by saying P.S. He's single. Now I'll horrify him again by saying P.S. He's not single!

SHHH! Don't tell, but he secretly loves the attention...

PHOTO BY JOHN HADELL

Diana
GODDESS of the HEART

WHEN I FIRST MET Diana and Her HusBand GeorGe, I Asked if they would Be MY FAiry GoDParents.

Diana Asked, "WHAT Does it entAiL?"

and I said, "To Love Me." Diana Quickly answered, "OH we Can Definitely Do THAT!"

I receive so MUCH Joy JUST sitting with Diana. She simply rADiAtes love. Her years of work with DEATH and Dying HAve opened Her HEArt Further, AM I AM SO GLAD SHe is Alive To Be of such service.

Diana retired, and promptly BeGan providing eldercAre services, with Her own company.

Her cAPAcity For loving is an inspiration.

I've leArned A lot ABout FAMily By observing Diana, and seeing How MUCH The HEArt Can HOLD.

When I think of Diana, I think of
Fresh peaches, women Artists, Adventure
Travel, Deep Gifts of Family, and the
replenishing Nature of the Feminine.

I think THAT Diana's Gifts come
From Her Faith, practice and personal
Growth work.
and THe eviDence of love MuLTiplied

Diana says, "I think THAT WHAT HAS
Sustained Me is THAT I stand on the
SHOULDERS of MY FAMILY THAT DID THese things
Before Me."

I want to Honor Her on These pages, and
Speak of Her spirit with SUCH

DEEP
PlEASURE

KATHryn

One of my first role models as a woman artist was Kathryn.

She seemed to exist so happily in a nonconformist world of her own making.

Her art and essence thrilled me, and inspired me to create my own artistic path. After Kathryn and I became friends, this is what I wrote about her:

"Woman who hears hawks dreaming. She carries gourds filled with colored pebbles and navigates swiftly through bamboo forests. Floating, climbing, flickering are some of her movements. She creates masks, ladders, and places for spirits to rest. She is shaman, teacher, Minnie Mouse.

Peanut Butter sandwiches in Between
visits to uranus. Invisible ink in her pens,
her soul creates constant ribbons of Art.
A treasured soul, A deep clay well,
LAughter flashing Bright. Stripes, polka
Dots, and the Mischief of elves. Her son
AJA, fellow of her forest, their footsteps
Blend in the sand. Five year old AJA asks
Me "Did you paint that for me when I WAS
one, or Before I WAS A number?"

Kathryn lives her creative life in
Maui with Her Gentle-soul surfer son, AJA.
She is an inspiration and A pleasure-
Bringer to our world.

Kathryn Oxman, 37, mask carver, Russian Hill:
Yes, because I have everything I want. I've been an adventuress, creative and courageous. The main thing is I've dealt with my fears so as not to live with a lot of fear.

Air of Adventure yes

anDreA
s c H e r

sHe reminds me vividly THAT pleasure reAlly (is) Around every corner.
THere is an Air of AdvenTure Around anDreA, and THe FeeLinG THAT anyTHinG couLD HAppen. THere is Also A sense of sAFety with anDreA. sAFety + AdvenTure Are A Most unusual ComBinATion!

sHe MAkes **superHero** necklAces, WHicH Are cHunky explosions of color anD LiGHT. THis is WHAT sHe wrote ABout one sHe MADe for me: "THere Are BiTs of oceAn in it, LAuGHTer, TanGerines and THe smell of FresH cut GrAss."

sHe is Also A pAinter of souL and DepTH. Her portrAits of PeopLe Are sTronG FiGures, noT AFraid to DisturD.

He ALso some times weArs A Tutu To THe superMArkeT

... I HAve 4 and THey HAve supernatural powers

ou can visit and See Her superHero necklAces
www. anDreAsCHer. com + pAintinGs!

recently, she called me and said,
"I'm going with my friend to Golden Gate Park to see the Dahlia Gardens. We're going to wear angel wings and ride a tandem bicycle."

Later she called me with a voice-mail recital of a truly miraculous day of sheer adventure.

i hope she publishes her photographs and writings of this day!

Andrea taught me how to play MAGPIE, a game she invented with the dictionary. You ask a question and open it randomly for the answer. This is actually how she came to work for my company!

She writes, creates, Dances and Makes Brilliant photographs too, all with Humility and Grace.

Andrea asked her question, which wa "What do I need to be more aware of?" The word she put her finger on in the Dictionary was SARK!

It is SCHer pleasure
to witness Andrea Gifting the world with JOY and Luminosity.

Thank you
Andrea!

LARRY

One of my dearest friends in the world is named Larry, and he is one of my pleasure mentors.

Larry is a genius-elf with an immense capacity for love and pleasure. I made a little book for him called "Larry's Open-Heart Adventure" and I said in it,

"He has Dancing Feet, a Musical Soul and a Rich Brain"

"He Chooses Friends Like Flowers, and Keeps vases All over The House"

it has little Heart Doors that you can open!

I wrote About Larry in my Book inspiration sandwich.

and Described How He Asked Me to Make a poster for Him About Being A Happy lawyer. So I Did, and This is What it said.

Larry Did Qvit THAT PArticular law practice, and went on To receive His pH.D. in public policy From Berkeley.

He is Also one of My PArcheesi partners and we play often, sometimes at an Age level of About 11. we used to THrow The Board and pieces As a type of CATHArsis, But stopped when we Broke a parcheesi Board.

HOW TO BE A HAPPY LAWYer

Qvit

BY SARK

Special note To lawyers: yes! I Believe you can Be a very Happy lawyer. A FACT, I Dare you!

ancient GAMe originally From india

and we never care who wins... THAT'S A lie!

I Always play with red, larry plays with Blve

Larry HAS an vncanny sense of Humor and effervescent sense of Life, and of Living. one NIGHT I WAS in My cottage, and He WAS in His Apartment Above. I Heard the window open, and Larry's voice
"Prepare To Hear 'KvBLA KHan'!" and He recited The entire poem loudly

For me and the entire neighborhood to enjoy.

I have also cried at his recitations of Yeats. When my dad died, Larry appointed himself my "grief slave," and let me cry voluminously on his shoulder.

He has summoned me to go on candlelit walks, dance in the rain and play parcheesi on our windy rooftop.

We share a garage, and have what we call "garage talk," which is essentially any conversation that takes place in the garage, and is usually odd or funny in some way. We also have funny arguments. Well, they're not all funny...

My friendship with Larry has restored my faith in succulent men, helped me to tell the truth faster, and made me laugh exceptionally hard. I receive such great pleasure from knowing Larry!

PLEASURE MENTORS

"THE CHURCH SAYS: THE BODY IS A SIN
SCIENCE SAYS: THE BODY IS A MACHINE
ADVERTISING SAYS: THE BODY IS A BUSINESS
THE BODY SAYS: I AM A FIESTA"
                        EDUARDO GALEANO

Cloud-Hidden, Whereabouts Unknown:
A Mountain Journal   By ALAN WATTS

Cultural Creatives   By PAUL H. RAY PH.D.
                     SHERRY RUTH ANDERSON PH.D.

Squeaky Chalk   By JOY SIKORSKI

My Grandfather's Blessings By RACHEL NAOMI REMEN M.D.

The Spirituality of Imperfection By ERNEST KURTZ
                          KATHERINE KETCHAM

WEB SIGHTS:
www.andreascher.com
www.aquariumage.com

"SOME OF YOU MIGHT HAVE THE DESIRE TO BECOME
THE BUDDHA OF THE AGE, MAITREYA, RADIATING
LOVE THROUGHOUT THE WORLD. INSTEAD, JUST
BE AN EARTHWORM WHO KNOWS ONLY TWO WORDS—
"LET GO, LET GO, LET GO"
                        A JAHN SUMEDHO

As we move through our lives,
we will all be taught by our pain.
Let's remember that pleasure is essential
too.
    Commit yourself to giving and
receiving pleasure, all of your days.
    Surround yourself with reminders
of the joy that you deserve to have
        J U S T   B Y   B e i n G
        Others are deeply touched by you,
even when you don't realize it.
    Thank you for bringing me pleasure
by reading my words and seeing my art.

    I will be here in San Francisco,
Traveling between pain and pleasure,
Sorrow and joy. I am practicing and
relearning everything I write about.
You can be sure I will be consciously
seeking pleasure!
    let's share our distinct pleasure at
Being alive together!
        l o v e,   SARK
San Francisco, California · December 2000

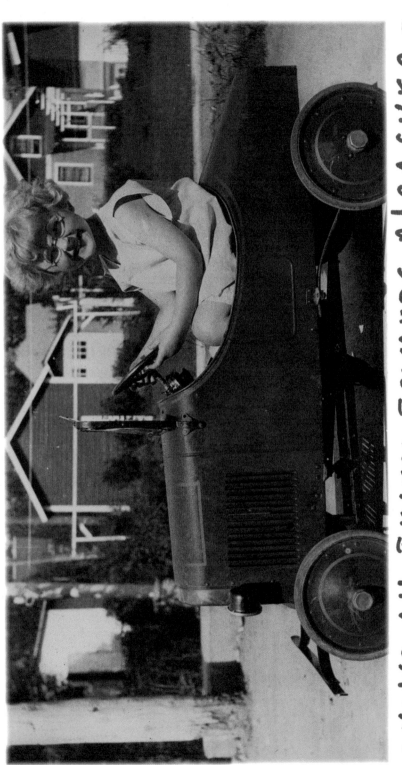

MAY WE All TRAVEL TOWARDS PLEASURE

in All of its FORMS

AND FIND OURSELVES WITH JOY IN THE MIDST

OF SORROW

WE ARE BUILT FOR PLEASURE, I ASSURE YOU

PHOTO OF MY DARLING MOM
"MARVELOUS MARJORIE"

So I send you, MY DEAR,
A BOWL of ripe Fruit that stays that
WAY until you're READY TO EAT it. I send you
A Flannel nightgown that Brushes the Floor,
and a paintbrush that whispers to you what to paint...

I send you A PATH in the WOODS THAT LEADS
to the GATE, WHICH LEADS to the SEA.

Then, A CARPET of Moss and a tea Party All set up!
You're the first guest to Arrive

I send you visions of
ladders To the new places in your soul, and slides
That lead out of the negative slots. I send you
new Knowledge of your resilience and Fortitude.
I send you special glue for the Broken places.
I send you Beauty in any ugliness you see, and the
ABility to truly respect your own pain.

TAKE A DEEP BREATH

I SeND YOU...
TuRQUOiSe WATer and pure WHite sanD...
I seND you the Discovery of A
Key on the Floor of the ocean...THis KEY
is encrusted with tiny Bits of sHells
THis is THe Key to Your Hidden
self. THe one you Feel cannot Be
seen. You Are SAFE.
let Your Hidden self Float Free...

I send you...

DAILY PRAYERS AND THE CONSTANCY
of love  *pray for surrender* love is always with us...

HARDER LAUGHTER AND MORE TEARS, *let's cry more*

RICH BUTTER COOKIES with no cALORIES
SHORTBREAD is GOOD

A SUDDEN, unplanned NAP *luxury nap*

I send you A DREAM in which you Fully realize
THAT none of us Are Alone, and THAT we Are All
SEEN, HEARD AND LOVED, JUST for BEING

I LIGHT A cANDLE in your name

We Are All succulent and BRAVE, HOLY,
ORDINARY, STUMBLING CREATURES

I SEND YOU LOVE

pleasurable

To reAch CAMP SARK

GO To: WWW. CAMPSARK-COM

or call: 415 397 7275 (SARK)

or write: P.O. Box 330039
SARKfrancisco CA
94133

CAll MY inspiration
PHONe Line (24 Hours)
415 546 3742 (epic)

"A PLACE TO BE HOW YOUActually Are"

Places + resources

To order
My First 5 Books:
A creative companion
inspiration sandwich
SARK'S Journal & Play! Book
Living Juicy
The Magic Cottage
Address Book

Call
Celestial
ARTS
1. 800. 841. BOOK
(2665)

Or
Go
To
www.Tenspeed.com

To order: Succulent Wild Woman
The Bodacious Book of Succulence
Change your Life Without Getting
out of Bed
Transformation Soup
For
More copies: EAT Mangoes NAKED
Call Simon & Schuster
1. 800. 223. 2336
Fax 1. 800. 943. 9831

* Call Special sales for
Special discounts for
Groups and Teachers
1. 800. 456. 6798

Or write Simon & Schuster at: 100 Front St.
riverside, New Jersey
08075

WWW. SIMONSAYS. COM
WWW. CAMPSARK. COM

YOU ARE MY GORGEOUS FRIEND!
YOU LISTEN DEEP TO ME... I
CAN tell you EMBARRASSING THINGS.
LET ME remind you of your HOLY
purpose, and the importance of
YOUR ORDINARY DAYS. I can REALLY
SEE YOU GROWING ...

Pleasure Pie — THANK YOU! THANK YOU! THANK YOU! THANK YOU!

every ingredient essential to the goodness
THANK YOU TO MY READERS

Zany — Awesome — Beatific — Creative — Delicious

BIG THANK YOU! TO CAMP SARK
Adrienne Steele
Brigette Scheel
Andrea Scher
Tanya Maboff
A TRIBUTE TO ACCOMPLISHMENT 2010 Tribute to SARK

Zoe Arielle — zen hospice
Adrienne + Ken + Zoe — Andrea + Tanya
Bigbo — Brigette — Bill + May-Tee
Bob — Bruce + Valerie + Declan
Kathy — Cecilia + Lulu — Chelsea — Charlie
Cathy — Craig — Claire
Debra + Steven David's — Doris
My Dem Dentists
Diana — Debbie — Eleanor — Emily Claire
Ecstatic — Eric Lesley + Alexa — Elissa
Fun — Gentle
To Families everywhere of choice + origin — Femail creations
GARY ROSENTHAL
Green world Mercantile — George + Diana
HILDEBRAND FAMILY
House restaurants — Gary + Angela + kids — Todd + Katie Houstons
Hope-filled
ISABEL COLLINS — illana — irving — insightful
illene
John + Robin — Jupiter — Jubilant
Jim + Sally Kennedy + kids
Joshua + Nick
John + Lois — Jennifer — Jackie
KATHRYN + AJA — Janice + Tony — Joe Brown
Karen Drucker — Katie Grant
Luchina Leigh — Liz — Leslie B.
Larry + Jackie + Rocky — Lindsey
Marsha — Maryann + Tim
Marjorie — Mardi — Maggie O
Marc + Cathy — Mackenzie + Julie
Lou Paget
Nicole + kids
neighbors: Sally, Michael, speaky, Tonya + Lea, Judy
Allow us to Be...
Open — Nurturing — Mellifluous — Loving — Kind
Patricia + Brandy — Penelope Smith — Pete's Cafe
Robyn Posin — Ray Davi — Roy
Q, Rare — Precious
Susan B — Sabrina — Stella
Salad-Like
Tanya + Ben — Tori
Tender
Vanessa — Vimala
U, Victorious
Wiss — Wayne — Yofe — Yes

inside THE BOOK Between THE Lines, WAS A PLACE to rest and ABSorB THE MAGIC

How COULD We ever Begin to PUT THE BOOK Down?

We LivE WiTH THE WORDS